BUILD THE PERFECT
BUG OUT VEHICLE

Creek Stewart

LR
LIVING READY BOOKS
IOLA, WISCONSIN
www.LivingReadyOnline.com

CONTENTS

Introduction 4

PHOTO COURTESY OF DAVID IEM

INTRODUCTION

AS MANY OF YOU KNOW, this title is the second in my *Build the Perfect Bug Out* series. My first book, *Build the Perfect Bug Out Bag*, started it all. It is a comprehensive no-nonsense guide to building a 72-hour disaster survival kit. I have designed each book to be completely independent, but you'll get more out of the series if you read them in order. Each one builds on the knowledge and skill sets discussed previously. I consider building a Bug Out Bag to be the first step in preparing for an inevitable large-scale disaster. The widespread success of that book confirms my gut feeling that a staggering number of people worldwide understand the need for practical preparedness and are actively seeking solid, quality information on the subject—minus the zombie hordes, political slants, and doomsday theories. Well, maybe a little bit of the zombie hordes, but none of the others.

At the end of the day, real disasters happen to real people on a regular basis. Mother Nature is a merciless adversary and it doesn't take a genius to realize that she is in control—always. In the past few years alone we've seen hurricanes, wildfires, floods, earthquakes, mud slides, and tornadoes devastate homes, cities, and regions both in the United States and abroad. Hurricane Sandy, dubbed Frankenstorm, unleashed

Build the Perfect Bug Out Bag

a fury on the upper East Coast that many experts believed to be nearly impossible. It is a statistical truth that natural disasters are larger, more frequent, and more violent than ever before in our history.

As if Mother Nature doesn't cause enough problems, we humans add in our own plethora of nightmarish events. From nuclear meltdowns to terrorist attacks and pandemic outbreaks, we are our own worst enemies.

Unfortunately, our two largest threats—Mother Nature and people—are extremely difficult to avoid. Sometimes, in order to survive disaster, our only option is to Bug Out and get away from it as fast as possible.

Natural disasters are larger, more frequent, and more violent than ever before in our history.

BUGGING OUT: DEFINED

The term *Bugging Out* refers to the decision to abandon your home due to an unexpected emergency situation, whether a natural disaster or one caused by man. The thought of having to evacuate your home due to a sudden and imminent threat is not at all unrealistic. The reality is that sudden and uncontrollable events of nature and man do happen. Natural disasters, such as hurricanes, storms, earthquakes, floods, and volcanic explosions can strike quickly with devastating effects on homes, vehicles, roads, medical facilities, and resource supply chains such as food, water, fuel, and electricity. Time and time again we have seen disasters strike

the United States and abroad, forcing tens of thousands of people from their homes with little warning. Unprepared and with no emergency plan, many of these people are left completely dependent on scavenging and handouts while living in makeshift shelters, fending for themselves in a time of complete chaos and disorder. In our unstable and unpredictable world economy, we would be foolish to think there is also no chance of a terrorist or military attack from forces domestic or foreign that could possibly force us to evacuate our own homes. An act of war is not the only threat from man. Dams burst, power plants go down, pipelines explode, oil spills occur, and other man-made structures and facilities can fail, resulting in disaster. Epidemics and outbreaks of disease could also warrant an evacuation.

We cannot control when, where, or how disasters strike. But we can control how prepared we are to deal with a disaster. There is a fine line between order and chaos, and sometimes that line can be measured in seconds. When every second counts, having a plan and the tools to see that plan through is crucial to survival. A Bug Out Vehicle (BOV) specifically chosen and outfitted with survival evacuation in mind may very well be your key to making it out alive.

Bug Out Vehicle

BUG OUT VEHICLE (BOV): DEFINED

Everyone has his or her own perception of the role for a BOV in a Bug Out scenario. It's a fairly subjective topic. For reasons I'll thoroughly explain later, I believe my definition is one of the more practical ones out there. Simply put, a BOV is a mode of transportation specifically and thoughtfully chosen based on budget, environment, and personal survival needs to transport you, your loved ones, and any necessary equipment and supplies to a predetermined destination (Bug Out Location) if and when the decision is made to Bug Out. Bug Out Vehicles are prepared in advance of disaster and are ready to leave at a moment's notice.

CHOOSING AND OUTFITTING THE PERFECT BOV

Whether you live in a high-rise loft in New York City or in the cornfields of Indiana, there is undisputable evidence that a disaster may one day force you to evacuate your home. As I always say, "It's not *if* but *when*." It happens to tens of thousands of people every year all over the world. Many do not make it out of the disaster zone in time and suffer incredible loss, including death. "Not making it" is due to either bad planning or bad luck, and you can't control luck. Although, I argue that the study of survival skills helps to "make your own luck." The what-ifs in life are someone else's reality, and your turn could be next. Just having a Bug Out Bag is not sufficient. All of the guns, bullets, food storage, survival skills, and seeds in the world will be of no use if you can't escape the disaster to begin with. If your Bug Out Plan does not include a BOV of some kind, then it is incomplete and, quite frankly, reckless.

Arguably, the most important aspect of surviving a sudden large-scale disaster is the ability to quickly, effectively, and safely get away from it. Only in the movies do people outrun a disaster on foot. In the real world, your best option is to "outwit" and "outsmart" a disaster by using every tool at your disposal. The disaster will always have the upper hand, but you can improve the odds.

The mode of transportation you choose should represent the best you can do with the resources you've been given. Do the best you can. Your life (and those of your family) may one day teeter on a BOV's ability to perform under horrific and unpredictable circumstances. Decisions you make now absolutely affect your options later.

Choosing a BOV is not an easy decision and should not be taken lightly. It is one of your most important survival tools. Any survival tool that your life depends on should be given thoughtful consideration. Choosing a BOV involves many factors. From budget to environment to family size, the list of deciding factors can be a little overwhelming.

In the following pages I will help you wade through all of these deciding factors. I'll discuss the "must haves" and "don't dos" along with the "whys" and "why nots." I'll detail important vehicle features and also outline items that should be packed in your BOV. I'll cover BOVs of all types—cars, trucks, bicycles, ATVs, boats, and even horses. I'll discuss city BOVs and those better suited for less urban environments. (And for all you guys out there, yes, there is a weapons section.) You'll also find BOV Highlight sections that showcase a wide variety of real-life BOVs other people (or companies) have built because it's always helpful (and fun) to see what other people are doing. Long story short, I will help you choose and outfit *your* perfect Bug Out Vehicle.

Let's get started. Mother Nature doesn't care about your busy schedule.

1 BOV MENTALITY

THIS SHORT CHAPTER SETS THE TONE for the entire book. You'll learn my thought process and reasoning behind the concept of a Bug Out Vehicle. Before we get into the nuts and bolts of choosing and outfitting a BOV, it's important to understand a BOV's role in your life.

I had a BOV before I knew what that phrase meant. For as long as I can remember, I've outfitted my vehicles with survival supplies and tools. From water to blankets to food and rescue tools, I've always prepared for the unexpected. In college, I kept an extra stash of breath mints in my BOV. Survival, no. Preparedness, yes. It's just the way I'm wired. With age and experience, my "BOV mentality" matured as well. Today, I have a well-grounded and practical thought process when it comes to the function of a BOV in my life.

POINT A TO POINT B

A BOV's primary function is to get you, your loved ones, and your supplies from ground zero to your Bug Out Location. It is a means to an end, not the end itself. I don't view a BOV as a long-term survival location. It is not a Bug Out Location. Some people view a BOV as the means of escape and also the final destination—a mobile Bug Out Location if you will. Are they right? Yes. Am I right? Yes. How? It's okay to have different opinions about a BOV. This book is my opinion. We can all learn from each other. My BOV's single purpose is to get me and my stuff from point A to point B.

NO EMOTIONAL ATTACHMENT

I love my BOV, but I love myself more. At the core of understanding what it means to Bug Out is the

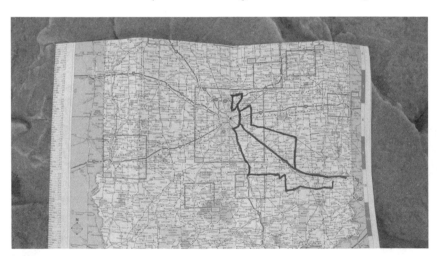

BOVs should get you from point A to point B.

Don't get too attached to your BOV; you may need to abandon it.

cold, harsh reality that you may have to leave "stuff" behind. You can't take everything. It just doesn't work that way. The first rule in raising farm animals for food is not to give them names. Don't name your BOV either. It's not a he or a she. It's an *it*. It doesn't feel pain or any kind of emotions. It doesn't get lonely, and it has no idea you even exist.

Disasters create some of the most chaotic, violent, and horrific circumstances on Earth. It's not hard to imagine that your BOV can only take you so far. For whatever reason, your vehicle might not be able to make the entire journey to your Bug Out Location. There are hundreds of reasons why, here are just a few:

- not enough fuel
- traffic jams
- impassible terrain
- vehicle malfunction or breakdown
- destroyed roads

You may very well have to leave your BOV behind and walk. This is exactly why I am not a proponent of investing your entire life savings in a BOV. It should be a vehicle that you can afford, but one that you can also afford to lose. The sooner you come to grips with the fact that you may have to abandon a BOV and everything you can't carry, the better. We will discuss some options, such as Bug Out Carts, for carrying extra gear on foot later in the book.

TO EACH THEIR OWN

You and I don't have the same Bug Out needs. No one does. Married, single, no kids, Brady bunch, disabilities, pets, city, urban, rural, coastal, inland, mountains, plains, warm, cold—there is a never-ending list of variables that forces us to make very unique BOV decisions. It is not a black-and-white decision. There are many more than fifty shades of gray. People love to voice strong opinions about BOVs. Your choice in a BOV only has to work for you, not the know-it-all on the survival forums or the belligerent commenter on YouTube.

READY OR NOT, HERE I COME

Bugging Out is like playing hide-and-seek with a disaster except you can't hear the disaster counting down its approach. Disasters can strike at any moment with little to no warning. Even with all of our modern technological indicators and gadgets, forewarning is a luxury and not a guarantee. Your BOV should be locked, loaded, and ready to rock at a moment's notice. It should need only two things: people and Bug Out Bags. You should not have to stop for anything in between ground zero and your Bug Out Location. Everything you

need to make the Bug Out Journey is pre-packed into (or very close to) the BOV. No exceptions.

AND THE AWARD FOR THE COOLEST BOV GOES TO...

Fight the urge to prioritize form before function. It's easy to let the idea of a cool-looking BOV cloud your best judgment. A disaster will not judge how your BOV looks, but it will judge how well it performs under pressure. Leave your ego at the door and focus on practical application. A common mistake I see people make is blowing their budget on bells and whistles that have no survival value, and then they don't have money for the important necessities. What would be more useful in a disaster Bug Out—flashy chrome rims or a 9,000-pound (4,000 kg) winch? If you end up with a practical BOV for your lifestyle that also looks cool, consider it a bonus.

LIFESTYLE DRIVEN

At the end of the day, BOV selection is driven by lifestyle. The lifestyle decisions you've made or plan to make will dictate what type of BOV you should choose. Let's discuss some of these factors in the next chapter.

BOV HIGHLIGHT: GM MILITARY M-1028 CUCV

VEHICLE MODEL: GENERAL MOTORS MILITARY M-1028 COMMERCIAL UTILITY CARGO VEHICLE (CUCV)

PRICE: $5,000 (AFTER A FEW FIXES AND UPGRADES, INCLUDING NEW TRANSMISSION)

PURCHASED ONLINE

MORE PHOTOS AT WWW.WILLOWHAVENOUTDOOR.COM

You are going to see this vehicle a lot throughout the book. I purchased it specifically for this project. It is a military surplus vehicle that I bought sight unseen from an online auction. It cost about five thousand dollars after a new transmission, ignition switch, a few electrical fixes/modifications, and two new 1000 CCA commercial batteries. This truck has power steering and brakes, a heater, and is rated to 1.25 tons. The 6.2L Detroit diesel engine is connected to a three-speed automatic transmission. It has a 20-gallon fuel tank and is four-wheel drive with manual locking front hubs.

I've owned several BOVs over the years, but never a retired military vehicle. This truck was built with combat support in mind and was probably used as a mobile command vehicle while in service. Writing this book was the perfect excuse for me to do something a bit different. The below photo is how it looked when I bought it. It is also the vehicle on the cover. You'll see how I chose to outfit and stock it in the coming chapters.

Creek's current BOV

2 LIFESTYLE FACTORS THAT AFFECT YOUR BOV

CHOOSING THE PERFECT BOV for your lifestyle involves many different factors, including some that aren't so exciting. Just as you would never choose a spouse based on looks alone, don't fall in love with a BOV's appearance. Oftentimes, "cool" isn't practical. Is it possible? Absolutely. But it's certainly not guaranteed and is actually so unimportant that it doesn't even make my list of deciding factors. When it comes to a BOV, function always trumps the cool factor.

As a guy, I certainly struggle with this. I want a cool-looking BOV just as much as the next guy, but I'm smart enough to understand that "cool" means zilch when it comes to life-saving benefits. After you get past the initial disappointment that you can't make a BOV decision based on looks alone, what follows are your core deciding factors.

WHAT CAN YOU AFFORD?

Yes, this first section is all about the Benjamins. A handful of companies design and manufacture vehicles I consider to be "dream" BOVs. Some of these are tailored specifically to the military and security industries. Others are targeted to outdoor adventure and off-road enthusiasts. All of them are expensive. Because of the price tag, high-end BOVs have an exclusive clientele. Take the UNICAT for example. At over half a million dollars, it is one of the most expensive and feature-rich BOVs on the planet. Its list of capabilities is staggering. Would I like to have it? Heck yeah. Can I afford it? Heck no. But I really like looking at it. And, I think the average consumer can learn a lot from BOVs like these, which is why I'll feature some dream BOVs, such as the UNICAT, throughout the book.

The reality is that for most of us, budget is the number-one deciding factor that affects our BOVs. It will control much of the decision-making process as you work within the confines of what you can afford. However, a little creativity can make a small

SURVIVAL QUICK TIP

If you can afford only one vehicle, I believe that using it as a BOV should be a major consideration when making that purchase. In a moment of crisis, no other purchasing criteria will matter.

budget go a long way. Throughout the book I will discuss several ways to add great features on a tight budget.

The good news is that if you can afford just one mode of transportation, you can afford a BOV. You don't necessarily need to purchase a separate vehicle that is solely dedicated to Bugging Out. The term *everyday driver* refers to a vehicle that you drive every day. Yes, your everyday driver can also be your BOV.

Having a BOV that is also your everyday driver does have certain advantages. First, if you drive it every day, you know that vehicle more intimately than you know a vehicle you drive only on occasion. This means you already know how it handles in rain, snow, mud, ice, and other conditions that you experience on a regular basis. You've used the drive-thru at the bank enough times to know what kind of clearances you need without

BOV HIGHLIGHT: UNICAT TERRACROSS 52 COMFORT

VEHICLE MODEL: UNICAT TERRACROSS 52 COMFORT
MANUFACTURER: UNICATAMERICAS, INC., WWW.UNICAT.COM
PRICE: $700,000 WITH ALL OPTIONS

The Unicat TerraCross 52 Comfort is designed, engineered, and built to sustain a family of four for two to three months in virtually any climate or terrain conditions. This vehicle is a classic example of a mobile Bug Out Location and its list of features is almost unbelievable. It is totally self-sufficient and meets the highest standards of safety, reliability, durability, capability, range, and comfort. It's fully winterized and can go from the heat of the Sahara to the cold of the North Pole, to the humidity of a rain forest. It's built on a 33,000 pound (15,000 kg) rated 4×4 chassis with a two-speed transfer case, six-speed automatic transmission, supplemental alternator, three-point kinematic stress-free body attachment, cab and seat air-ride suspension, cab-to-body passage, ultra light, highly insulated rigid composite body panels, burglar proof, scratch proof, double paned, thermally insulated windows with mosquito netting and black-out blinds, fully equipped kitchen and bathroom, systems-wide redundancy, plenty of outside and inside storage, 200 gallons fuel (1,600 mi range), 110 gallons water and on-board desalination/decontamination unit, diesel hot water and space heating, electrical - 3 ×123w solar panels, 3,000w inverter/charger, 6 × 210ah AGM batteries, 8Kw genset, electronics - 2 ×

having to get out and check. You are familiar with the vehicle's sounds and know its quirks and limitations. You have a working relationship with your everyday driver that will always be more intimate than with a vehicle you use much less frequently. You also know the vehicle is in good working order.

For a long time, I had a 1972 Ford Bronco dedicated as my BOV. I rarely drove it and I can't tell you how many times the battery was dead when I tried to start it. This is a classic example of how an awesome dedicated BOV can end up being worthless in a time of immediate need. Dedicated BOVs absolutely require routine attention and maintenance.

WHERE DO YOU LIVE?

Where you live weighs in heavily on your BOV decision. It's not practical for someone in Manhattan who

UNICAT TerraCross 52 Comfort Bug Out Vehicle

TV/DVD, 2 × AM/FM CD/iPod, CB radio, BGAN global communications, 2 × GPS, propane - 2 × 30 pound (13 kg) cylinders, military-grade first aid kit, full complement of tools and spare parts, two folding bicycles, two-person scooter, 15' inflatable Zodiac w/15hp outboard, two-person kayak, fishing gear, hunting and protection gear, four folding chairs, two tables, and two hammocks. Aside from being a phenomenal adventure travel vehicle, it also makes the list as a dream BOV. Even though most can't afford a vehicle like this, we can still learn a great deal by studying its list of features.

Bug Out Cargo Bike by Yuba Bicycles (detailed later)

has limited space and no parking to buy a large SUV. If a large-scale disaster strikes Manhattan, do you really think everyone is going to be able to drive out anyway? They'd have better luck catching a seat on a flying pig. This is true for *all* large cities. An urbanite's best BOV option may be a pedal-powered cargo bike. It can fit in an apartment, carry a Bug Out Bag and a few other necessities (like Fido), and weave in and out of jam-packed traffic lines that plug limited exit routes. On the other hand, someone living in a more rural area doesn't have the same set of limitations and would definitely be better served with a four-wheel drive vehicle of his or her choice.

Similarly, weather in northern Minnesota poses an entirely different set of concerns than the weather in south Florida. This may seem like common sense, but one of the worst decisions I've ever made was when I bought a two-wheel drive truck in Indiana. That thing would get stuck on wet pavement. A new two-wheel drive was the same price as a used four-wheel drive, and I let form trump function. Rookie mistake.

Later chapters discuss a huge variety of BOVs and include the pros and cons of each along with who should consider them and why.

WHO'S RIDING WITH YOU?

Who you live with affects your BOV options. Not only must your BOV safely fit the people and animals you intend to save, but it must also accommodate their Bug Out Bags and any additional supplies you intend to pack, such as strollers, wagons, fuel,

Too much gear for this BOV

water, wheelchair(s), etc. Yes, a large SUV will fit six people. But will it fit six people, a child seat, a golden retriever, five Bug Out Bags, a stroller, and a cooler of food? I don't know. Even if the answer is no, the vehicle might still work. Additional exterior storage might be necessary. We will discuss exterior storage options later in the book. Sometimes it's the simple oversights that have the worst consequences. Preplanning is critical.

WHERE ARE YOU GOING?

I believe that no Bug Out Plan is complete without a predetermined survival destination—your Bug Out Location (BOL). The details of this location may affect the type of BOV you should choose. I know a guy whose BOL is on an island in the ocean. He actually has two BOVs. One is a truck

to get him to the dock. The other is a sailboat to get him to the island. Obviously, his BOL dictates his BOV. I also have a friend whose BOL is at the end of a fourteen-mile road (road is an exaggeration) near the top of a mountain that is only passable with a four-wheel drive vehicle. His vehicle must have four-wheel drive. A BOL that's one thousand miles away (not recommended) may require a more fuel-efficient vehicle than one that is two hundred miles away. Does your BOL limit the kind of BOV you can choose?

THREE PACKING STRATEGIES

We will soon begin to discuss and consider a variety of products, tools and supplies that one should consider when packing a BOV. Before we do, you need to start defining what kind of BOV packer you are. There are three strategies to consider and none of them are wrong. It will help if you decide early on in the process which one you are most comfortable with.

Build Strategy 1: BOB Heavy

This category is for those of you who feel you have pretty much everything you need for a 72-hour Bug Out packed in your Bug Out Bag. You do not see a need to pack more survival tools, food, water, or supplies in your BOV. After all, that's what a Bug Out Bag is for, right? A BOV is simply a mode of transportation from point A to point B, nothing more and nothing less.

Build Strategy 2: BOV Heavy

This category is for those of you who see a BOV as another *layer* of security and choose to pack redundant survival tools, food, water, and supplies inside even though you already have those items packed into your Bug Out Bag. You have decided to reserve your Bug Out Bag as a last-ditch effort and don't want to break into it until you are officially on foot. In essence, you look at your BOV as another really big Bug Out Bag. You plan on using the resources in your BOV first before you open your Bug Out Bag. Note: This is the category I fall into.

Build Strategy 3: BOB/BOV Hybrid

Most people will find themselves most comfortable with this strategy. For some reason or other (maybe time or budget) you don't want to pack a bunch of redundant items in your BOV that you already have in your Bug Out Bag. You may decide to pack some redundant items but certainly not everything. Your BOV isn't an entirely independent second layer, but rather a great spot to pack *extra* stuff that you couldn't fit into your Bug Out Bag, like more water, a bigger shelter, and some extra clothes. You have no problem with using items out of your Bug Out Bag while traveling in your BOV.

SUMMARY

Your lifestyle will help you choose a general type of vehicle to use for Bugging Out. You need a vehicle you can afford, works with your environment, accommodates your full load (of people and supplies), and gets you where you need to go.

But lifestyle details aren't the only factors to consider when choosing a BOV. The attributes of the BOV itself are equally important. Two people can choose the same type of BOV but outfit them to perform very differently. The devil is in the details. The next chapter covers the attributes I believe every BOV must have.

3 ▶ BOV ESSENTIAL ATTRIBUTES

THE VAST MAJORITY OF READERS will choose a car, truck, or SUV for a BOV. Ninety-five percent of this book revolves around those vehicles. Some, however, are considering bicycles, motorcycles, boats, or some other type of transportation either as a primary or maybe a secondary backup BOV that will be loaded and stored on or inside of a primary BOV.

It's important to have goals when building a BOV. Ideally, any primary BOV choice meets the following list of essential attributes:

- good working order
- four-wheel drive
- necessary storage
- distance capable
- water-crossing clearance
- readily available replacement parts
- the ability to blend in

Don't let this list stress you out. It's designed for a best possible scenario, and few of us will be able to meet every requirement perfectly, and some requirements might not be met at all. This chapter will discuss each attribute in more detail.

GOOD WORKING ORDER

The first and most essential attribute is that your BOV must be in good working order. Nothing else matters if your vehicle isn't reliable. If you can't trust it to make the journey to your Bug Out Location (BOL), either remedy the issue(s) or get a different vehicle. There is no excuse for a person who takes preparedness seriously to have a BOV in disrepair. All BOVs require routine maintenance to keep them reliable. The following list details the most important routine checks and balances.

Oil Change: Contaminants such as dust, grime, moisture, and metal shavings increase engine wear and tear. Change your oil and filter every three thousand miles or every three months, whichever comes first.

Air Filter: Clogged air filters result in lower fuel mileage and power loss. A general rule of thumb is to replace your filter when it looks dirty and full of crud. Trying to clean it is pointless. Spend a few bucks and get a new one. Check, and replace if necessary, during each oil change.

Clogged air filter

Fuel Filter: Clogged fuel filters place unnecessary strain on the fuel pump, which results in loss of power and poor performance. Fuel filters trap rust and debris from the fuel tank. I replace mine annually.

Brakes: Do you get a physical each year at the doctor's office? If not, you should. And, so should your car. This vehicle "checkup" should include a brake inspection. Follow the mechanic's advice to keep them in good working order.

Wiper Blades: Have you ever been in a snow- or rainstorm with bad or broken wiper blades? Even worse is after a storm when cars in front of you are spraying up dirty road water. Bad blades can be flat-out dangerous. Driving through and away from a disaster (and potentially off-road) will almost certainly require that your windshield wipers are in good repair. Don't procrastinate, change them when necessary.

Fluids: Just as our body needs proper hydration to function at peak performance, your BOV needs fluids as well. Make sure brake, transmission, radiator, windshield washer, and oil levels are always where they should be. These should be checked and adjusted during your routine oil change.

NEWER MODERN VEHICLE VS. OLDER PRE-1980S MODEL

When researching BOVs, you will quickly find advocates of older pre-1980s vehicles. Some survivalists are pro older vehicles for two main reasons. First, older vehicles are typically less complicated to troubleshoot and repair in the field. Second, they have fewer (some none at all) electronic parts that could be susceptible to failure during a potential electromagnetic pulse (EMP), which I discuss in detail later in the book.

Which one should you choose? Well, that depends on you. The fact is that older vehicles are not as dependable as newer ones. Even when these older vehicles were new, they weren't even close to being as dependable as newer modern vehicles (1990s and newer). In my humble opinion, threat of EMP is the only reason to consider an older pre-1980s vehicle. There is no BOV that can cover you from 100 percent of the potential threats. You have to ask yourself what you are preparing for and make decisions based on those answers. If EMP is at the top of your list, you may want to consider an older and less electronic-dependent vehicle. Otherwise, a more modern vehicle might be a better choice, especially if you aren't a practiced mechanic.

Need new blades?

Maintain fluid levels.

Taking an alternate off-road route

Tires: Tires are your car's hiking boots. They should be routinely inspected and rotated—including your spare. If there's a slow leak, get it fixed. No one wants to spend their hard-earned money on expensive new tires, but if your BOV needs new tires, buy them.

Belts: All worn or damaged drive belts should be promptly replaced. Signs of wear and tear can include cracks and a slick glazed appearance.

A BOV in good health ranks number one on your list of priorities. Make sure your BOV is reliable before you invest time or money on any other BOV preparedness efforts. Of course, driving in disaster conditions can take a toll on your BOV and cause problems for even the best maintained vehicle. Chapter five details vehicle maintenance items to keep in your BOV.

FOUR-WHEEL DRIVE

If a large-scale disaster forces sudden evacuation, there's a high probability that you can expect less-than-perfect driving conditions. Here's a short list of potential obstacles:

- flooding
- natural and man-made debris such as trees, limbs, and building rubble
- mud/mudslides
- driving on medians and road

shoulders to bypass traffic jams or roadblocks

- heavy snow
- road damage, such as large crevices and shifting pavement
- traveling or camping off the beaten path to avoid confrontation with others

In my opinion, four-wheel drive is a BOV necessity if you can afford it. I've owned two-wheel drive cars and trucks, and they are absolutely inferior to vehicles with four-wheel drive. Not all four-wheel drive systems are the same. Automobile manufacturers have actually made it confusing with all of the fancy marketing names they've invented in an attempt to differentiate their drive systems from competitors.

To understand four-wheel drive, also called 4×4 and 4WD, it's important to understand how it's different from all-wheel drive (AWD). To the uninformed, you might think AWD and 4WD are the same. Well, they are and they aren't.

All-Wheel Drive (AWD)

It's easiest to look at AWD as a light-duty 4WD with no driver options. The engine supplies power to all of the wheels all of the time. The driver typically has no input. AWD is designed to be used on roads in bad weather versus being used for actual off-road travel. Most vehicles that have AWD are cars, although some light-duty SUVs now come with AWD.

Four-Wheel Drive (4WD)

A true 4WD vehicle has a 4LO or 4LOW setting. The driver can engage this setting to increase torque for exceptionally difficult terrain. However, even true 4WD systems have variations.

Part-Time 4WD: In this system, the rear two wheels typically power the vehicle when 4WD is not activated. The two front wheels join the party when the driver engages 4WD. Older trucks have manual locking hubs that require the operator to physically turn a knob on the front wheels. Modern vehicles don't require this step.

Automatic 4WD: Automatic 4WD is similar to part-time 4WD except that the vehicle automatically engages the front two wheels when it senses loss of traction in one of the rear wheels. The driver does not have to tell it to engage and, depending on the make, doesn't have a choice.

Full-Time 4WD: This simply means that the engine will send power to all wheels all the time. The drivers cannot switch between two-wheel and four-wheel drive. This is similar to the AWD listed above except 4WD vehicles are typically built with more ro-

4LOW option

Manual locking hubs on front tires

Interior 4WD selection buttons

bust and rugged systems with gearing that is better suited for true off-road conditions.

Creek's Preference: I prefer a part-time 4WD system. This system has a 4LO setting option for true off-roading needs. I also like being able to control when 4WD is engaged. The part-time and automatic systems are more fuel efficient than full-time systems because power feeds all four wheels only when necessary. There is no need to waste fuel on powering all four wheels when you don't need it.

Limiting your choices to only on-road travel is a risky decision and may leave you with few options in a sudden large-scale evacuation. Chapter six is dedicated to outfitting your vehicle with equipment to help any type of BOV with off-road travel.

NECESSARY STORAGE

Your BOV must have enough storage space to safely carry you, your loved ones, and each passenger's Bug Out Bag. This is an absolute minimum. Additional room to store extra supplies, such as water and tools, for the journey is highly recommended as you will see once we get into the outfitting chapters. Space and solutions for storing fuel are also critical. There are a variety of creative interior and exterior storage options to consider for vehicles with limited space.

Many of these options are discussed in chapter nine.

DISTANCE CAPABLE

If you talk to anyone who has evacuated a large-scale disaster by vehicle, that person will tell you the importance of having a vehicle that can make it a long distance. History repeatedly reports that fuel becomes virtually impossible to source in the midst of a large-scale disaster evacuation. If you do not have enough fuel to make your Bug Out Journey when the disaster strikes, you probably aren't going to get any more. Gas stations may be either closed for the same reason you are evacuating, not functioning due to lack of power or other disaster-related interruption, already jammed with lines of frustrated and desperate evacuees, or simply out of gas altogether. Your BOV should be capable of making the trip to your Bug Out Location without stopping to refuel. And, because disaster-related delays and detours are expected, you should consider extra fuel storage in your vehicle.

Running out of fuel will be one of your greatest threats. The catch-22 is that most extremely fuel-efficient ve-

BOV FUEL: GASOLINE OR DIESEL?

A diesel engine has two main advantages over gasoline, but these don't necessarily mean you should choose diesel. First, diesel engines are simpler. Consequently, they are more reliable and tend to last longer, and most mechanics agree they are easier to troubleshoot and repair. Second, diesel engines can be converted to use vegetable and waste oils. Many survival-minded individuals like the idea of being able to use these types of fuels versus traditional fuel supplies in the event of a long-term collapse. However, modern vehicle engines are incredibly dependable. Fierce competition among car companies has resulted in gasoline engines that can be expected to run upwards of 200,000 miles. And, gasoline is much more popular and easier to find. Your chances of scavenging gasoline during a disaster Bug Out Journey are higher than finding diesel. I chose a diesel because I am designing this dedicated BOV to be more of a long-term collapse BOV and have plans to make the vegetable oil conversion. All of my other BOVs have been gasoline. It is also important to note that diesel has a much longer shelf life than gasoline. Many survival-minded individuals store fuel, and this can also influence one's vehicle choices.

Overall, are you more concerned about a short-term disaster Bug Out or a long-term societal collapse?

hicles do not make ideal BOVs. You must choose the right BOV and fuel storage combination to get the job done for your particular lifestyle and needs. Only you know how far your Bug Out Location is from your permanent residence.

WATER-CROSSING CLEARANCE

Flooding is one of the most common occurrences and obstacles in many natural and man-made disasters. From blown dams and bursting water pipelines to overwhelmed ditches and heavy rains, flooding can stop traffic in an instant. I have seen cars stall out in as little as 12 inches (30cm) of floodwater. Floodwater can short-circuit vital vehicle functions, clog the air intake, and clog the exhaust. Any one of these can cause a BOV to stall. A BOV should have a minimum of 24 inches (60cm) of clearance to the air intake. On a modern vehicle, most air intakes are located just inside the front grill. Chapter six discusses options for increasing a vehicle's clearance when crossing water.

READILY AVAILABLE PARTS

I like the idea of choosing a very popular, mass-produced model vehicle as a BOV. This helps to ensure that replacement and repair parts are more readily available should the need arise. In times of normalcy when In-ternet, phones, and shipping carriers are not interrupted, it may not be hard to find a replacement part for an oddball domestic or import vehicle, but that could be a completely different story in times of disaster or unrest. You may have to resort to junkyards, local vendors, or barter. Parts for popular vehicles will be easier to find and also less expensive. Also, these types of vehicles blend into a crowd better, which brings us to the final attribute.

THE ABILITY TO BLEND IN

There is a fine line between being prepared and not appearing to be prepared. Blending in during a disaster Bug Out certainly has advantages. One could argue that the most average-looking BOV is the most strategically attractive. It doesn't grab attention. It doesn't stand out. It doesn't scream, "I have food, water, and survival supplies—come and get it." Desperate people take desperate measures, and staying on the down low during a disaster Bug Out is a smart strategy. I'll be the first to admit, my truck featured on the cover and throughout this book stands out in a crowd of typical vehicles. But I just couldn't in good conscience write a book about BOVs and not give you some cool Bug Out eye candy. The accessories and urban

Creek's camouflaged BOV

camouflage look great in photos, but in reality may draw unwanted attention. But you have to admit that you like the pictures.

Earth tones like tans, browns, and greens are great BOV colors as opposed to bright and flashy reds and yellows. Not only do earth tones attract less attention in a sea of chaos, but the time may come when you wish to disappear completely. An earth tone vehicle is much easier to camouflage. Whether you want to camp overnight and wish to remain anonymous or simply need to escape and evade, camouflaging your BOV can be very useful. Chapter eight has some vehicle camo ideas.

SUMMARY

The whole point of this book is to simplify the overwhelming task of building the perfect BOV. Perfect is a very subjective term. You have to accept the fact that it's impossible to prepare a perfect plan (and vehicle) for an imperfect world. It's impossible to predict all the details of any potential disaster Bug Out. Choose a vehicle that meets as many of the above requirements as possible within your budget and move on. An imperfect BOV that's ready to go is far better than a perfect BOV that isn't ready (or exists only in your dreams) when disaster strikes.

4 BOV SURVIVAL SUPPLIES

ONCE A VEHICLE PLATFORM IS CHOSEN, it's time to outfit it with Bug Out gear. I look at my BOV as a huge mobile Bug Out Bag. Theoretically, even if you have nothing at all packed in your BOV, you should still have enough in your Bug Out Bag (BOB) to get you through three days of independent survival. This is the point in your build when you really need to decide which BOB/BOV Build Strategy that I discussed in chapter two you are going to choose when it comes to survival supplies. This strategy will play a big role as you gather and assemble your BOV supplies. Some of you who are on a tight budget need to hear this next sentence.

If you can't afford to outfit your BOV exactly as I've outlined in this book, it's okay.

But, your BOB needs to be top notch. One could argue that it's not necessary to pack anything at all in a BOV except your BOB, and I wouldn't necessarily disagree. However, as I discussed in chapter two, I don't take that approach. I like the idea of outfitting a BOV with extra survival supplies and tools. Doing so creates multiple layers of preparedness. Your BOV becomes a new layer of readiness between your BOB and your Bug Out Location. My plan is to utilize the extra resources in my BOV first and keep my BOB as a fully intact Plan B. A BOB should always be a last-ditch effort.

The next several chapters highlight different categories to consider when outfitting and prepping a BOV. This chapter will focus on survival supplies. Most of these items will be redundant to what you already have packed in a BOB, but with a BOV twist because the limitations for size

SURVIVAL QUICK TIP

You must be prepared to abandon your BOV and everything in it. You may have to complete your Bug Out Journey on foot with only your Bug Out Bag. You have to take this fact into account when stocking your BOV. I'll also discuss some Bug Out Cart options in chapter fourteen if you have to abandon your BOV and still want to carry extra supplies.

Repurposed Deer Cart to carry Bug Out supplies (from The Sportsman's Guide)

and weight aren't as stringent. It's about creating layers of preparedness.

BUG OUT BAG(S)

All survival supplies should already be packed inside your BOV. Your Bug Out Bag(s) is the only exception (except for extreme hot and cold climates, which I discuss later). It's stored in your house. Disasters create very chaotic and confusing scenarios, and it's easy to overlook even obvious steps when in a panicked rush. Don't forget your BOB. A BOB is a self-contained, 72-hour disaster kit that contains all the supplies necessary to get you and your family through three days of independent survival. If you have to travel by foot, it is indisputably your most important resource. If you haven't yet read my first book in this series, *Build the Perfect Bug Out Bag*, consider adding it to your survival library. Because I've chosen the BOV Heavy Build Strategy, all of the survival resources listed below are in addition to what is already packed in a BOB.

BOV SHELTER

For some, a BOV is a shelter in and of itself. Large SUVs, vans, and mobile homes make perfect temporary shelters for unpredictable overnights on a Bug Out Journey. Extra storage room in a BOV gives you the opportunity to include more elaborate sheltering items than what you may have room for in a BOB.

Extra Clothing and Cold Weather Gear

Hypothermia is the number-one outdoor killer in the United States. You can die in as little as three hours without proper shelter in extreme conditions. The ability to regulate core body

Bug Out Bag packed and ready to go

Plastic tote with extra cold weather gear

Additional BOV tarp canopy

temperature during a cold weather Bug Out is critical. It's not hard to imagine that you might have to shelter overnight during a Bug Out Journey. Heat shouldn't be a problem while the vehicle is running, but it would be crazy to waste vital fuel just to keep the heater warm. Cold weather survival gear is essential for those who live in four-season regions. Packing these items in a BOB can be difficult

SURVIVAL QUICK TIP

Quickly boost your sleeping bag cold rating with only 3.8 ounces (108g)! Purchasing a low-degree rated, lightweight sleeping bag for extreme cold presents two big challenges: They can be expensive and bulky. However, you can add an Adventure Medical Products SOL Emergency Bivvy to any sleeping bag and drastically improve the cold rating. The SOL Bivvy weighs only 3.8 ounces (108g) and costs under twenty dollars. It's basically a sleeping bag made out of emergency survival blanket material. It reflects up to 80 percent of your body heat. Layer it inside of an average-rated bag to create great cold weather sleeping setup.

Adventure Medical Products SOL Emergency Bivvy

SOL Bivvy layered inside of lightweight sleeping bag

Creek's camo clothing

Rooftop tent from www.arbusa.com

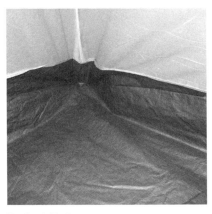

Bathtub Bottom

because of the bulk, so including them in a BOV makes perfect sense. Some items to consider are

- extra blankets
- cold weather hats and gloves
- lower degree sleeping bags
- extra emergency survival blankets / bivvy

Even though I carry an extra set of clothing in my Bug Out Bag, I have also added one to my BOV. This set includes camouflage pants, shirt, hat, gloves, jacket, and face mask. I may never need a full camo outfit, but I'd rather have it and not need it than need it and not have it. There's a little bit of Rambo in all of us survival types.

Shelter Options

Sleeping in a BOV may sound ideal, but it's not always practical. This is the one advantage that large enclosed BOVs have over smaller alternatives. If your BOV doesn't have interior sleeping space or you aren't towing a camper of some sort, you'll want to think about how you might handle an unexpected night on the road. Extra storage space in a BOV allows for you to pack larger and more substantial sheltering options if you want to use something more extravagant than what is in your BOB. The use of integrated vehicle tents is a growing trend among adventure travelers and represents an excellent BOV shelter system.

Integrated vehicle tents typically mount on the roof of a car, truck, or van. Selecting your campsite is as simple as parking the car. This option also frees up valuable storage space inside the vehicle. Bedding items can typically store inside the collapsed tent as well. I've even seen these mounted to the top of dedicated Bug Out Trailers, which we will discuss later. These are definitely one of the more expensive shelter options but certainly have their advantages.

Traditional camping tents are the most affordable shelter option. With those, the selection is mind-boggling. Below is a list of features to look for when selecting a Bug Out Tent:

- Earth tone or camouflage: Give yourself the option to be discreet if you need to be.
- Bathtub bottom: A bathtub bottom extends a few inches up the walls all the way around the tent and is great for wet and rainy conditions.
- Rain fly: Make sure your tent has a rain fly—some don't.
- Free standing: Make sure your tent can be configured without the use of guy lines if necessary.

BOV WATER

Water is at the top of the list when it comes to survival priorities. You can't have too much! You should already have three liters of fresh drinking water packed in your BOB, but you should absolutely pack more water in your BOV. I suggest packing a minimum of one gallon per person per day in addition to what is already in your BOB.

One of the most popular questions I get at Willow Haven is whether or not one should store water in a

SURVIVAL QUICK TIP

Extremities, such as fingers and toes, are most vulnerable to cold. Pack hand and foot warmers that can be activated to generate long-lasting warm heat when you need it most. They are lightweight and inexpensive and perfect for extra vehicle storage when space is tight in your BOB.

HotHands brand hand and foot warmers from www.hothandsdirect.com

Large multi-person free-standing tent

Commercial bottled water options

Single bottles marked with expiration date and stored under the seat

BOV year-round. I personally don't like storing water in my BOV during extreme heat and extreme cold. Extreme heat can leech some nasty stuff out of plastic containers (even food grade), and extreme cold can obviously freeze and damage containers. Outside of the dead of winter and summer, I keep water storage in my BOV. During extreme months I keep it inside, ready to grab and go near my BOB.

There are countless different ways to store water in a BOV. Here are my favorite three options:

Easiest: Commercially Bottled Water

Want the easiest BOV water storage option? Just buy bottled water. Bottled water typically has an expiration date of at least two years, and the shrink-wrapped cases are easy to stack and store. Loose bottles can also be stashed in small nooks and crannies to utilize every square inch of available storage. If the expiration date is only printed on the case packaging be sure to also write it on the individual bottles with a permanent marker.

Cheapest: Bottle Your Own Water

Almost any empty plastic resealable drinking container makes for ideal extra water storage. Make sure they are food grade containers. Two-liter pop bottles are my container of choice.

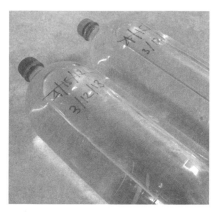

Repurposed two-liter soda bottles filled with tap water and marked with fill date

Six-gallon BPA-free water containers from Walmart

Even though I don't drink soda, friends and family are happy to donate more than I can ever use. Thoroughly wash empty bottles and fill with either municipal or well water. Before you seal the lids, put in two drops of regular 4-6 percent household bleach per one liter of water. Make sure it's regular with no added scents or softeners. This will give the water a storage life of at least one year. I change my BOV water storage annually.

Bulk: Bulk Water Containers

There are literally hundreds of commercially available bulk water storage containers on the market. Again, make sure any container you use for water storage is food grade. If you've got the storage space, more water is always better. In addition to some commercially bottled water, I keep two six-gallon water totes in my BOV that I picked up in the camping section at Walmart for around ten dollars each.

HOUSEHOLD BLEACH

Bleach can also be used to purify questionable water as well. Just remember that you have to be 21 years old to drink. Use 2 drops of regular 4-6 percent household bleach per 1 liter of water. Hence, 21. That equals 8 drops per gallon. The water must be clear to start with, not murky or muddy. Once the bleach is added, you need to wait thirty minutes. And don't forget the threads! Be sure to splash some bleach water around the threads of your container if it has a lid. Waterborne pathogens could be trapped there.

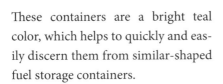

Disposable lighters, several ferro rods, and matches in waterproof container

WetFire brand fire tinder

These containers are a bright teal color, which helps to quickly and easily discern them from similar-shaped fuel storage containers.

BOV FIRE

You may not plan on stopping during a disaster Bug Out, but plans can change, and it's important to prepare for a variety of setbacks. You may at some point need to start a fire. Fire is a critical survival tool that can cook/warm food, boil and purify additional water, signal for rescue, and regulate core body temperature. I suggest keeping a very basic fire kit in your BOV in additional to the one packed in your Bug Out Bag. Your BOV fire kit should include the following.

Ignition Device

Unless you want to start a fire by rubbing two sticks together, you'll need to pack an ignition device. In fact, pack several. A couple of disposable lighters and a ferro rod should be all you'll ever need. Lighters will not function properly in extreme cold or when they get wet. Ferro rods, also called metal matches, and modern-day flint and steel, will create sparks to ignite fire tinder in virtually any weather condition. I really like the Light My Fire brand ferro rods.

Fire Tinder

You should always pack good fire tinder in any fire kit you make. Store bought fire tinders, such as WetFire, are proven winners. However, you can make your own tinder at home and it will cost you virtually nothing. We call them PET balls at Willow Haven. They are simply cotton balls mixed with petroleum jelly. A big dollop of petroleum jelly smeared onto a cotton ball is one of the best fire-starting tinders on planet Earth. It will ignite almost immediately with just one strike of a ferro rod and will burn upward of five to seven minutes. Make twenty-five of these and store them in a resealable bag in your fire kit.

PET Balls: Cotton balls mixed with petroleum jelly

Fire Kindling

When building a fire, you ignite fire tinder (PET balls) first. Fire kindling is used to grow the fire. It is typically larger and more substantial. Disaster conditions can render almost all available natural fire kindling useless. Don't depend on gathering kindling from the wild unless you have no other choice. I recommend two types of kindling:

Fatwood: Fatwood is the word used to describe the resin-rich heartwood of the pine tree. Pine resin collects in the joints between the main trunk and the limbs but also settles in the stump and roots when the pine trees are harvested for other purposes. This pine resin saturated wood is extremely flammable and has been used since the beginning of time for fire starting. It's now harvested commercially and sold in bundles at most home and garden stores. It makes perfect kindling even in wet and windy conditions, and just one PET ball will easily ignite a few sticks of

Package of fatwood fire kindling

Homemade fire-starting eggs

Fire Eggs Step 1: Fill pressed fiber egg carton cups with sawdust.

Fire Eggs Step 2: Fill each cup with melted wax.

Fire Eggs Step 3: Tear apart the finished fire eggs.

fatwood. These can then be used to ignite larger sticks and logs.

Fire Eggs: I use homemade fire eggs almost exclusively to quickly and easily start fires at home and at Willow Haven. They are extremely effective and easy to make. You'll first need an empty pressed-fiber egg carton. Don't use the Styrofoam ones. Fill each of the empty cups with sawdust and then cover the sawdust with melted wax. Any kind of candle wax will work. Even old crayons will work. You can find big candles at Goodwill for pennies. After the wax cools, tear apart the fire eggs and keep them in a resealable bag until you need them. Just light a corner and these little guys will burn hot for at least fifteen minutes.

Firewood

This may seem like overkill to some people, but my goal when bugging out in a BOV is to be a completely self-contained survival unit. I prefer to have everything I think I will need packed in my BOV. This includes a small stash of firewood. Not only do I have the tinder and the kindling, but I also have the wood necessary to build at least a couple of really good fires. Rather than pack actual split wood, I choose to go with a case of Duraflame's Roasting Logs. These individually packaged logs can be lit without the use of additional tinder or kindling. All you have to do is light the ends of the wrappers. The Roasting Logs are specially formulated for roasting and cooking from 100 percent renewable resources. They are compact and easy to transport and store. One case of Roasting Logs is good for four to six small campfires and takes up considerably less space than the same equivalent in split firewood.

Light a corner of the fire egg to use.

BOV FOOD

Because of the extreme weather changes here in Indiana, I store extra BOV food items during peak months in a waterproof bucket next to my BOV water and BOB in a hallway leading out the door. The shelf life of any food drastically decreases with prolonged exposure to extreme heat, no matter what it says on the package. When packing food in your Bug Out Bag, weight and size is of utmost importance. You don't necessarily have those concerns when packing your BOV. Below are the most important criteria for BOV food:

Long shelf life: Choose foods with a minimum shelf life of one year. Make your life easy by choosing foods with long shelf lives so you don't have to constantly change out expiring food items. Ideally, just one review and exchange of perishable items should be necessary annually.

Case of Duraflame Roasting Logs from www.duraflame.com

Duraflame Roasting Logs, fire-starting tools, and tinder packed in waterproof plastic five-gallon bucket

Open and Eat Meals: Time, energy, and resource conservation are top priorities. Choose meals that do not require extensive preparation. The last thing you want to do is pull over to prepare meals.

High-Calorie Foods: Survival food is about calories. Don't pack shallow food. Make sure your BOV food puts fuel on the human furnace.

At the time of writing this book I am on a version of the Paleo Diet, which pretty much means I eat only meat and vegetables. Luckily, that still includes bacon or else it would be extremely difficult. This also means that I find myself fantasizing about having to Bug Out just to gorge myself on the food stores I have in my BOV. My point is that you shouldn't get too caught up in following strict diet guidelines when packing for a Bug Out. Foods that meet the Bug Out Food criteria above aren't necessarily diet friendly. For me at least, these include two basic categories of food items:

Canned Foods

Canned foods are a perfect BOV survival food ration. They meet all of the above criteria. From canned meats such as Vienna sausages and SPAM to hearty raviolis and canned pastas, there's no lack of suitable options. And, I've never met a kid who doesn't like every single one of them. They have a long shelf life, they are packed with calories, and they require very little to zero preparation.

Civilian Military Meals Ready to Eat (MREs)

Soldiers are issued MREs while serving in the field. Essentially, these are completely self-contained meal kits. They typically contain an entrée, a condiment pack, a large cracker, a

Variety of Bug Out canned foods

Civilian Military Meals Ready to Eat

small desert, and a water-activated chemical heat source. Often, the outer package serves as the cooking and heating container. These meal kits are time-tested in the field and are a very reliable and nutritious BOB food ration. They contain the most calories of any food item listed in this chapter—typically one thousand-plus calories per meal.

The government restricts the commercial sale of official Military MREs. You can still find them on ebay.com, in Army/Navy surplus stores, and at gun shows. However, these are typically overpriced. The better option is to buy what are called "Commercial or Civilian MREs," which are very similar to the military version and often produced by the same manufacturers that sell direct to the military. I don't recommend buying MREs on ebay.com—there

are just too many imposters and it can be difficult to tell the difference. Below is a list of reputable companies from which to purchase commercial MREs. You can compare the prices and kits and make your own choice. I have purchased from each of them with no issues.

- mredepot.com (sells a variety of MRE manufacturers)
- Mrestar.com
- ameriqual.com (U.S. Military MRE Contractor)

A sample MRE purchased from mrestar.com includes:

- 8 oz. entrée (e.g., lentil stew with potatoes and ham)
- 2 oz. dry fruit (e.g., banana, pineapple, papaya, etc.)
- 2 oz. raisins & mix nuts (e.g., raisins, peanuts, almonds, sunflower seeds)
- 2 oz. sugar cookies

SURVIVAL QUICK TIP

Don't forget the can opener! As a backup, pick up a military-style P-38 can opener at your local Army/Navy surplus. They are only about an 1½ inches (4cm) and can go right on your BOV key ring.

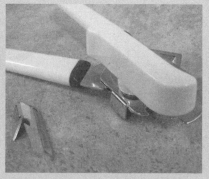

Regular can opener and small P-38 military-style version

Canned foods and MREs stored in plastic, food-grade bucket

Five-year-old and heavily used GSI Outdoors Stainless Glacier Bottle Cup

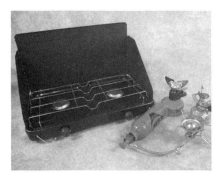

Sampling of canister stoves and larger tabletop propane stove

- Drink mix (e.g., orange flavor with vitamin C)
- Accessory pack (spoon, coffee, sugar, creamer, salt, pepper, napkin, moist towel)

If you don't heed my advice and instead pack food that needs a heat source for warming and/or cooking, you'll need a camp stove and a basic cooking kit. My cooking kit consists of only two items: a GSI Outdoors Stainless Glacier Bottle Cup, which nests on Nalgene-sized bottles, and a Light My Fire brand spork. For larger families, one might consider a larger pot. Dehydrated meals should be the most complex meal you plan on preparing during a Bug Out Journey, and a simple pot to boil water is all you will need.

You'll have to decide whether you want to pack an additional set than what may already be in your Bug Out Bag. I have a full BOV kit in addition to my BOB, but as I've mentioned, I prefer for my BOB to remain a complete kit until I have to travel by foot.

Building a fire to cook is sufficient, but not always practical. Fires are time-consuming, fuel-consuming, and indiscreet. Consider packing a lightweight backpacking canister stove, a solid tab fuel stove from Esbit (like I carry in my Bug Out Bag), or a tabletop propane stove. Tabletop pro-

Adventure First Aid Kit 1.0

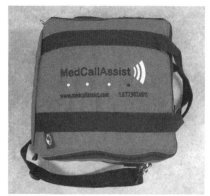

MedCall Kit for BOV

pane stoves are popular for car camping and remote cabins. If you go this route, fuel canisters should be kept out of the vehicle during months of extreme heat.

BOV FIRST AID AND HYGIENE

First aid and hygiene are closely related. Poor hygiene can lead to first aid issues. In order to stay healthy and/or efficiently heal existing wounds, proper hygiene is imperative. It's also not hard to imagine the need for first aid supplies during a disaster evacuation.

BOV First Aid

The number-one public service to become overwhelmed during disaster emergencies is 911. Emergency responders and medical facilities become immediately clogged with disaster-related incidents. For far too many people, calling 911 is a Bug Out Strategy. You cannot depend on emergency medical service during a large-scale disaster. It just isn't smart and it certainly isn't a plan. A better strategy is to do the absolute best you can to prepare for a variety of potential first aid related issues independently. This involves having an extensive Bug Out first aid kit as well as professional first aid training.

Remember, prescription medications and an extra pair of glasses (if necessary) should already be securely packed in your BOB.

I purchased the first aid kits for both my BOB and BOV and then added to them according to my needs. My base Bug Out Bag first aid kit is the Adventure Medical Kits Adventure First Aid 1.0 and my base BOV first aid kit is the MedCallKit from www.medcallassist.com. Another great source for extensive medical kits is Chinook Medical Gear, Inc. at www.chinookmed.com.

BUG OUT FIRST AID KIT COMPARISON

BUG OUT BAG FIRST AID KIT

- [ ] 10 Antiseptic Wipes
- [ ] 15 Assorted Adhesive Bandages (1" × 3")
- [ ] 5 Sterile Strips
- [ ] 4 Sterile Gauze Pads (3" × 3")
- [ ] 1 Sterile Gauze Roll Bandage (2" × 2 yards)
- [ ] 1 Medical Tape (1" × 10 yards)
- [ ] 2 Moleskin Patches (4" × 5")
- [ ] Sunscreen: Small Tube or Towelettes
- [ ] Lip Balm
- [ ] 1 Elastic Wrap Bandage: 2 yards (2m)
- [ ] Antibiotic Ointment: 1 small tube or 2 single use packets
- [ ] 4 Alcohol Swabs
- [ ] 5 Ibuprofen Pills, 200mg
- [ ] 5 Antihistamine Pills, 25mg (Diphenhydramine Hydrochloride)
- [ ] 5 Acetaminophen Pills, 200mg
- [ ] 3 Aspirin Pills, 325mg
- [ ] 2 Imodium Pills, 125mg (Simethicone)
- [ ] 3 Antiemetic Pills, 50mg (Dramamine) (dimenhydrinate)
- [ ] Baby Vitamins
- [ ] Visine Eye Wash
- [ ] 2 Rubber Gloves
- [ ] Tweezers (for splinters and ticks)
- [ ] 5 Safety Pins
- [ ] Insect Repellant
- [ ] Mirror
- [ ] Emergency Survival Blanket (reflect body heat to prevent hypothermia)

BUG OUT VEHICLE FIRST AID KIT

- [ ] 1 z-pak or 6 Pills Azithromycin, 250mg
- [ ] 14 Ciprofloxacin Pills, 500mg
- [ ] 14 Sulfamethoxazole/trimethoprim DS Tablets
- [ ] 28 Cephalexin Pills, 500mg
- [ ] Triple Antibiotic Ointment: 10 Individual 1gm-Packets
- [ ] Gentamicin Ophthalmic Solution: 5 cc 1 tube
- [ ] 40 Ibuprofen Pills, 200mg
- [ ] 40 Acetaminophen Pills, 500mg
- [ ] 10 Cimetidine Pills, 800mg
- [ ] 12 Bismuth Tablets
- [ ] 1 oz. Tube Tucks Hemorrhoidal Ointment
- [ ] 20 Loperamide Pills, 2mg (Imodium)
- [ ] 5 Bisacodyl Pills (Senna-Lax Tablets)
- [ ] Ondansetron (Zofran) 4mg : One 4mg-vial with 6 doses
- [ ] 1 Toothache Kit (Red Cross Toothache Kit one step temp tooth filling)
- [ ] Epinephrine 1mg vial: 1 vial with 3 doses
- [ ] 2 Safety Syringes (Monojet insulin 1cc safety syringes)

- [ ] 4 oz. Bottle Guaifenesin-DM
- [ ] 15gm Tube Tolnaftate Cream 1%
- [ ] 18 Throat Lozenges
- [ ] 15gm Tube Triamcinolone Cream .1%
- [ ] 15 Diphenhydramine Pills, 25mg
- [ ] 10 Loratadine D pills, 10mg
- [ ] Cough Drops: 1 roll (8 drops)
- [ ] 6 SteriStrips (1 pack)
- [ ] 1 Pack Assorted Adhesive Bandages
- [ ] 20 Cotton Swabs
- [ ] 5 Tongue Depressors
- [ ] 4 Adaptic Pads
- [ ] 2 Tegaderm Bandages (2" × 3")
- [ ] 10 Gauze Pads (4" × 4")
- [ ] 2 Petrolatum Gauze Pads (3" × 9")
- [ ] 1 roll, 1"-wide Paper Tape
- [ ] 1 roll, 1"-wide Cloth Tape
- [ ] 1 roll, 4"-wide Kerlix Gauze
- [ ] 1 roll, 4"-wide Elastic Wrap Bandage
- [ ] 5 Large Safety Pins
- [ ] 1 Z-fold Hemostatic Bandage (QuikClot)
- [ ] 8 Rubber Gloves
- [ ] 1 Skin Stapler with 15 Staples
- [ ] 1 Skin Stapler Remover
- [ ] 1 Tube of Wound Glue
- [ ] 1 Set of Splinter Forceps
- [ ] 1 Set of Iris Scissors
- [ ] 1 Pen Light

- [ ] 1 Tube of Lip Balm with Sunblock
- [ ] 4 packets of SPF 30 Sunblock
- [ ] 1 Magnifying Glass
- [ ] 1 Set of Nail Clippers
- [ ] 1, 18g needle
- [ ] 5 Moleskin Precut Pads
- [ ] 1 Set of 8" (20cm) Paramedic Shears
- [ ] 1 Monoject Curved Tip Irrigation Syringe
- [ ] Urine Catheter Kit
- [ ] Lidocaine 1% 50cc
- [ ] Suture Set
- [ ] IV Kit (Start Kit, 18g Catheter, Admin Set and 1L Saline)
- [ ] SAM Splint
- [ ] Combat Application Tourniquet
- [ ] Insect Repellant
- [ ] Mirror
- [ ] Emergency Survival Blanket (reflect body heat to prevent hypothermia)

I'm sure you can piece together your own BOV medical kit and save money, but buying them complete is a great option for busy schedules. The lists I've provided can at least give you a good benchmark to design your own kit.

It goes without saying that proper training is required to use several of the aforementioned items. The common mistake I see when packing first aid kits is when people include products beyond their training. Unless you've got the money and space to spare, including kit items beyond your level of medical training should not be a high priority. A huge variety of first aid training classes (including Wilderness First Aid) can be found in your local area at www.redcross.org. EMT training is also a great survival knowledge base supplement.

BOV Motion Sickness: If anyone in your Bug Out Crew gets motion sickness, don't forget to include Dramamine in your first aid kit. There's nothing that can make a Bug Out Journey more miserable than nausea associated with motion sickness.

BOV Hygiene

Bug Out Hygiene, especially in a small space like a vehicle, is critical. Disasters have an uncanny reputation for creating incredibly unhygienic environments. Polluted flood water, sewage disruption, waste disposal interruption, and power outages all encourage a breeding ground for illness, disease, and infection. Human and animal waste (feces, urine, blood, and other bodily fluids) represent some of our greatest health threats. Entire civilizations have gone virtually extinct due to misunderstanding and underestimating the dangers of human waste. Even today, in developing countries, lack of

PRESCRIPTION MEDS AND BUGGING OUT

You'll notice in my extensive BOV medical kit that I have several prescription medicines. I believe it is important to develop a good relationship with a survival-minded physician. This is a doctor who understands your concerns for needing "just in case" Bug Out prescription medications—whether they are simply more of the medications you already take or extra ones such as antibiotics. If your doctor does not share your same concerns for a potential disaster scenario, I would suggest getting a different doctor. MedCallAssist.com, who is the supplier of my kit, also offers several medications with their kits.

proper sanitation is a leading cause of sickness and death.

I recommend a dedicated BOV hygiene kit that includes the following items. This kit can be modified to fit virtually any kind of BOV.

Paper Towels and Toilet Paper: I'll admit, I have a weakness when it comes to paper towels. I use a lot of them and enjoy it. I don't skimp. I prefer disposable paper towels over the cloth alternatives. A big fat roll of paper towels is a great addition to a vehicle hygiene kit. In my opinion, you can never have too many. They are perfect for a myriad of clean-up scenarios. Toilet paper is pretty self-explanatory. Nature may call during your Bug Out Journey and you should be prepared to answer. Keep these items protected in waterproof bags—you may have to go potty in the rain! I use SealLine Dry Bags from cascadedesigns.com/sealline.

These dry bags are incredibly durable and can be used to keep a variety of Bug Out Gear protected from moisture and water. You can also use larger resealable plastic bags.

Disinfecting and Cleaning Supplies: I suggest keeping a smaller pail inside of your main hygiene kit. In this pail, I keep disinfecting wipes, a bottle of hand sanitizer, a 2.5-gallon resealable bag, twelve disposable nitrile gloves, a small bottle of regular

Paper towels and toilet paper in SealLine Dry Bags

Small disinfecting pail with lid

Extra personal hygiene kit kept in BOV with First Aid and Hygiene supplies

BOV waste bucket with lid and contractor-grade trash bags

All BOV first aid and hygiene products in plastic storage tote

household bleach (I rebottled this into a Nalgene travel container to fit), and a scrubber sponge. The disinfecting wipes are perfect for quickly wiping down surfaces, and the pail and bleach can be used to mix a bleach-water solution for larger jobs if necessary. The gloves are good for protecting your hands from the bleach solution as well as whatever disgusting substance you might be cleaning up. The bleach can also be used to purify additional water if necessary. A sealable pail keeps these items separated from the rest of your hygiene kit.

Personal Hygiene: I highly recommend having a small stash of extra personal hygiene products in addition to what is already in your BOB. This includes the following:

SURVIVAL QUICK TIP

Did you know a tampon makes excellent fire-starting tinder? The cottony fibers of a tampon will ignite with just one small spark from a ferro rod. I actually keep a couple packed in my fire kit just for that purpose!

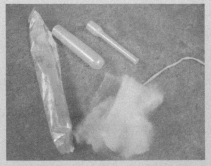

Cotton fibers of tampon separated and ready to receive spark

- anti-bacterial baby wipes, perfect for quick waterless baths if necessary
- extra clothing (having a full extra outfit is a good idea; this includes socks, underwear, shirt and pants)
- toothbrush, toothpaste, dental floss
- small camp towel (I use a Lightload Towel from www.ultralighttowels.com)
- small soap/soap sheets
- hand sanitizer
- toilet paper (already mentioned and packed with paper towels)
- feminine hygiene products
- diapers (infants and incontinent adults)

Garbage Bags/Resealable Bags: I can't stress enough the importance of being able to contain and properly dispose of trash and waste. You may be forced to store a variety of waste products in your vehicle while en route to your Bug Out Location. Garbage bags and large resealable bags are perfect for isolating anything from food waste to dirty diapers. Large 2.5-gallon resealable watertight freezer bags can be purchased from most grocery stores. A dedicated multiuse waste bucket isn't a bad idea either. I use a clearly marked five-gallon bucket that has a roll of fifty-five gallon heavy contractor-grade trash bags inside.

SUMMARY

When I teach survival courses at Willow Haven, I focus on what I call The Core Four. These are Shelter, Water, Fire, and Food. These four categories, along with First Aid and Hygiene, are your top priorities when beefing up a BOV basic survival supplies kit.

SURVIVAL QUICK TIP

Looking for a hassle-free on-the-go Bug Out toilet option? This GO Anywhere Toilet Kit is the *only* biodegradable solution that traps, encapsulates, deodorizes, and breaks down human waste with a NASA-developed gelling agent. Use it, seal it, and toss it in the normal trash. Go to cleanwaste.com/go-anywhere-trial-pack to get a free trial pack.

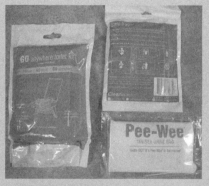

GO Anywhere Toilet Kit

EVEN IF YOUR BOV STARTS the journey in perfect running order, a disaster Bug Out presents a minefield of potential maintenance issues. The ability to make expedient field repairs for common vehicle break-down problems is a necessary component to any BOV Bug Out kit. From punctured tires and dead batteries to lost keys and broken belts, the most popular causes for breakdowns can be solved with a little preplanning and a few basic spare parts and tools. Below are some categories to consider when stocking vehicle maintenance preps.

THREE MOST COMMON CAUSES FOR BOV BREAKDOWNS
Flat or Punctured Tire

Road rubble from building or industrial debris and off-road hazards, such as thorns (locust tree) or nails, can easily puncture a tire. The first line of defense is a spare, preferably full size. This is the quickest and easiest solution to getting back on the road. Spare tires, especially full size, can take up a lot of space. I've chosen to mount mine to the exterior using the Warrior Products Universal Spare Tire Mount for quick and easy access. Many cars come with smaller space-saving spares often referred to as "donuts." If you don't have room for a full-size spare, consider picking up an extra donut at a local junkyard. They are normally only a few bucks. Donuts aren't meant for high speeds or long distances, so having a "spare donut" for your "spare donut" is recommended. This may seem obvious, but it's important to routinely check your spare tire's air pressure. I had a flat once on the expressway and went to put on my spare only to find out that it was also flat. Needless to say, I learned a big lesson.

A nice floor jack is a recommended upgrade to the stock scissor or piston jack that comes standard in most vehicles. Floor jacks are easier and faster to use. They are also much

Flat tire

Unexpected screw in tire

Warrior Products Universal Spare Tire Mount from www.warriorproducts.com

Spare "donut" compared to full-size tire

Floor jack (left) and stock scissor and piston jacks (right)

Hi-Lift Jack lifting Creek's BOV

more stable, especially on uneven or off-road surfaces. They typically come with a much more durable tire iron as well. If not, consider buying one of those as well.

Vehicles with significant ground clearance will need what's called a Hi-Lift Jack from www.hi-lift.com. Hi-Lift Jacks are designed specifically to bridge this high clearance gap and are used extensively by off-road enthusiasts in harsh environments all over the world. They are a rugged versatile tool that not only lift but also pull, push, winch, and clamp. I've even used my Hi-Lift Jack to pull fence posts.

I also suggest packing a square 24" × 24" (61cm × 61cm) of ¾-inch (2cm) thick piece of plywood (also mentioned in chapter six). This can be used to place under a jack to prevent it from sinking into soft gravel, mud, or sand. Without this, you'll be forced to improvise with what you can find at your location, which might not be much. Expect the unexpected.

Hi-Lift Off-Road Jack mounted to Creek's BOV

Board base under vehicle jack

Jack sinking in sand

Fix-A-Flat aerosol tire inflator and Slime Tire Sealant

Your last line of defense in fixing a flat tire should include some Fix-A-Flat, a tire repair kit, and a 12-volt electric air compressor. Fix-A-Flat is designed to seal small punctures and inflate a tire long enough to relocate and seek a more permanent fix. Flat tires seem to only happen at the worst possible time, and a quick shot of Fix-A-Flat or Slime Tire Sealant may be just what you need in order to find a safer spot to change or repair the tire. Learn more about these products at fixaflat.com and slime.com.

Tire punctures from nails, wire, thorns, and glass don't necessarily destroy a tire. Repairing that puncture may be your best option. An inexpensive tire repair kit combined with a 12-volt mini air compressor allows you to quickly fix simple punctures in the field. Twelve-volt mini compressors simply plug into a cigarette lighter port and run using the power from a vehicle's electrical system. They can be used to inflate tires, air mattresses, and even inflatable canoes and life rafts.

Fix-A-Flat Brand 12-volt mini air compressor

Solar battery trickle charger mounted to exterior of BOV

L-brackets to secure battery and inverter

Dead Battery

Car batteries rarely give an owner early warning signs for failure. One day they can start your car and the next day be dead as a doornail. Something as simple as leaving the lights on can drain a brand-new battery in just a few hours. Or, a battery can just go bad after years of use. Either way, preparing to deal with battery trouble is a good idea.

An Emergency Kit (detailed later in this chapter) with jumper cables is an absolute Bug Out necessity. Getting a jump from another evacuee or member of your Bug Out Convoy may be all you need to get back up and running. Sometimes, though, it's not that easy. Batteries have a life and you never know when they will die. I keep a spare new battery in my BOV. It's expensive (a hundred dollars) but worth it in peace of mind. I've hooked up a solar battery trickle charger from AutoZone to keep this spare topped off at all times. In a pinch, you can also use this spare battery with an inverter to run small electrical items such as lights, a laptop, or battery chargers. I also attached L-brackets to the floor to keep the battery from shifting around during travel.

Jump-start boost units are also available. These are often charged from your cigarette lighter during normal travel and can be used to jump a dead battery if you have no other options. This obviously isn't necessary if you keep a spare battery, but they are still pretty cool products.

Keys: Lost, Locked In, or Dead Remote

Though not technically a breakdown, lost or locked-in keys is statistically one of the most common reasons for calling roadside assistance. Especially with older BOVs like mine, locking your keys inside is an easy mistake to make. I'll admit to doing it on more than one occasion. Disasters manufacture very chaotic environments, and it's not hard at all to imagine misplacing or losing a set of BOV keys in the hustle and bustle of getting out the door or even during a rushed stop midway through the journey. An easy solution is to keep a spare set of keys in a magnetic hide-a-key case under the bumper or frame of your vehicle.

Many modern vehicles have a key fob instead of a traditional key. Oftentimes, these fobs are battery dependent. It is a well-known fact that batteries fail only when you need them most, so be sure to keep a spare key fob battery on hand if your vehicle uses this technology. I've heard stories of people with these fobs not even being able to open their car door due to a dead fob battery.

Mobile jump-start boost unit

Magnetic hide-a-key case

Fancy key fob that does not use a traditional key

SPARE PARTS AND FLUIDS

Everything man-made will eventually break and oftentimes will do so without warning or good reason. Routine maintenance, as discussed previously, will keep most of the catastrophic malfunctions at bay, but you still must prepare for the worst. Keeping a selection of spare parts and fluids in your BOV can turn a life-threatening breakdown into just an annoying hiccup. Below is a list of the most common spare parts and fluids to consider:

Most common spare parts:
- battery (already mentioned)
- keys (already mentioned)
- spare tire (already mentioned)
- engine belts (fan belt/serpentine)
- fuses
- thermostat

Most common extra fluids:
- fuel (detailed extensively in chapter nine)
- engine oil
- power steering fluid
- wiper fluid
- engine coolant (though water or even urine will work in an emergency)
- transmission fluid
- brake fluid

TOOLS

A small toolbox with commonly used tools will be necessary for almost any impromptu field repair. And, you just never know when a good tool will come in handy. Below is a minimum list. You can supplement this list as you feel necessary.

BOV Toolbox
Screwdrivers
- flat head: three different sizes (small, medium, large)
- Phillips: three different sizes (small, medium, large)

A few extra fluids

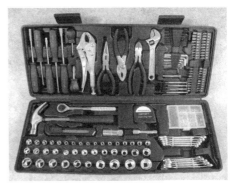

BOV toolbox

Spare BOV parts

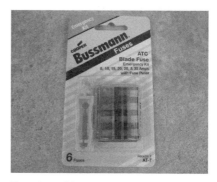

Extra box of fuses

Pliers
- needle nose
- vise grips
- channel locks
- slip joint

Socket set that includes both standard and metric sizes

Wrench set that includes both standard and metric sizes

General Use Maintenance Resources

Besides tools, the below assortment of miscellaneous supplies can certainly come in handy for improvised field repairs that might require creative solutions.

Duct Tape: Do I really need an explanation for why to pack one roll (or twelve) of duct tape? Entire books have been written about the multifunctional uses for duct tape. Trust me, pack a few rolls.

Plastic Zip Ties: Zip ties are perfect for gear repairs or organizing rope, wire, and cables. Keep a variety of sizes on hand.

Thick-Gauge Bailing Wire: You never know when you might have to secure a loose or broken exhaust pipe. Thick-gauge wire has a variety of uses.

Metal Strapping: This has a similar purpose as thick-gauge wire so only one or the other is necessary. This is typically found in the plumbing section of hardware stores.

Hand-Pump Siphon: Did you know that some gas can spouts won't fit into the hole of your car's tank? A siphon can help you fill your tank but also scavenge fuel from other sources if necessary.

Hose Clamps: When you need a hose clamp, nothing else will quite work.

Repair Manual: Very detailed and extensive repair manuals are available for many vehicles. These are typically much more helpful than the service manual that comes with the vehicle.

Consider packing one of these just in case. A popular manual supplier is Haynes.com.

Work Gloves: Ever tried changing a flat tire in the middle of winter or clearing brush with a hand saw while winching a truck through harsh terrain? If you ever have to, you'll wish you had a nice pair of all-purpose gloves. Gloves not only keep your hands clean, but can also protect them from cuts, scratches, and inclement weather. I prefer an all-purpose tactical-style glove that works well for a variety of tasks including handling tools, driving, shooting, reloading magazines, and sifting through Bug Out Gear. I've chosen the Reactor Hard Knuckle from Hatch. Hatch specializes in the military and law enforcement sectors. The Reactor gloves have built-in hard PVC knuckles and foam padding, but are still flexible enough to use with more detailed tasks.

Duct tape, plastic zip ties, metal strapping, and hose clamps

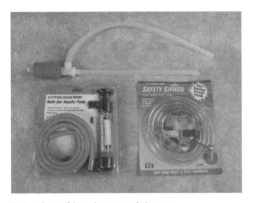

Selection of hand-pump siphons

EMERGENCY KIT

It's a good idea to keep a standard emergency kit in every vehicle, whether it's your BOV or not. This kit should include a variety of basic emergency items. You can assemble these à la cart on your own, but sometimes they can be cheaper (and certainly easier) to buy in a prepackaged kit. This 110-piece kit is available at bellautomotive.com for only around

Reactor Hard Knuckle Gloves from www.hatch-corp.com

thirty dollars and includes all the basics. Notice it contains some duplicate items previously mentioned, but it doesn't hurt to have extras, and it's nice to have all of these items located in one easy-to-find bag or tote. The following list identifies the emergency kit item followed by the recommended quantity for your kit:

- 8-foot jumper cable: 1
- cloth blanket: 1
- 12-foot (3.6m) tow rope: 1
- 2-in-1 screwdriver: 1
- tire sealant: 1
- adjustable wrench: 1
- cable ties: 30
- flashlight: 1
- AA batteries: 2
- help sign: 1
- 18" tie down: 1
- rain poncho: 1
- 64-piece first aid kit: 1
- car care guide: 1
- accident document guide: 1
- pair of knit gloves: 1
- emergency contact info: 1
- carry bag: 1

No vehicle emergency kit would be complete without a fire extinguisher. I've added a dry chemical MaxOut fire extinguisher available from h3rperformance.com. This particular extinguisher is very effective against automotive fires because it smothers liquid fires without conducting electricity back to the operator. It is also rated effective against wood, paper, rubber, and plastics, which makes it ideal for a BOL once you arrive as well. Their quick-release billet aluminum mounting brackets provide a rock-solid attachment to virtually any surface to keep it in place during bumpy evacuation conditions.

The last tool I've added to this emergency kit is on my key ring. The

H3R Performance MaxOut Automotive Fire Extinguisher with billet aluminum mounting bracket

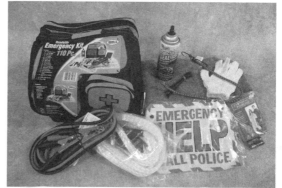

Bellautomotive.com 110-piece emergency kit

H3R Performance MaxOut Automotive Fire Extinguisher mounted in BOV

ResQMe 2-in-1 Key Chain Rescue Tool from www.resqme.com

ResQMe tool is designed as a quick access dual-purpose emergency tool. It has a hook blade for cutting through seatbelts and also a striking function designed for shattering windows. You may need this to escape if the earthquake you're running from flips your BOV in a watery ditch, trapping everyone inside.

SUMMARY

I know, there's a lot of items mentioned in this chapter. It can feel a bit overwhelming to someone just starting out. Don't expect to assemble these items in one weekend or even one month. Piece together the vehicle maintenance portion of your BOV over time as your budget allows. You may already have many of these items and it's just a matter of organizing them in your vehicle. This is the first place to start. Then, prioritize other items that you need to acquire.

SURVIVAL QUICK TIP

Add fire starter to the long list of duct tape's multifunctional uses. Tear it into thin strips and make an "urban bird's nest." When exposed to an open flame, such as a disposable lighter, a bird's nest of duct tape can be excellent tinder to get a fire going in adverse conditions.

Duct tape bird's nest on fire

6 OFF-ROAD TRAVEL

WE'VE ALREADY DISCUSSED the importance of the four-wheel drive option in a BOV. Sometimes, however, even the best off-road vehicles need a little help. Whether you've chosen a 4×4 vehicle or not, many of the tools and modifications in this chapter can be essential to off-road travel, especially in inclement weather. Some of these items may seem over-the-top, but we are preparing for a worst-case scenario so I've tried not to leave any stone unturned. This chapter includes both tools and vehicle modifications that can assist with a huge variety of off-roading scenarios and obstacles; all of which should be expected in a potential Bug Out.

TIRE SELECTION

Tires are expensive. It's hard to justify getting new tires when you don't need them. However, the next time your vehicle is due for tires, take Bugging Out into consideration. Tires are basically hiking boots for your BOV. You would never wear slick loafers to hike difficult terrain. Low-tread road tires are ideal for driving on nice clean blacktop roads, but become less than desirable in snowy, sandy, or muddy conditions. At the same time, super-treaded tires can severely affect gas mileage and even make a vehicle difficult to control at high speeds. The happy medium is a moderately

treaded tire that's good both on and off the road. Below are my top three all-terrain, on and off-road tire picks:

- Interco Tire Corporation: Model SS-M16
- BFGoodrich All-Terrain T/A KO
- Goodyear Wrangler AT/S

Because tires are so important, I changed out the stock boots on my surplus M1028 pickup to a set of ridiculously awesome Super Swampers from www.intercotire.com. This also required a wheel upgrade, which I found on Craigslist for under one hundred dollars.

A slightly larger tire can also give you a few extra inches of ground clearance. Ground clearance is important for many reasons. First, the more clearance you have, the less likely you are to damage the underside of your vehicle by accidentally running over rubble or branches. As we discussed earlier, ground clearance is also important when fording high water. Every inch counts when it comes to keeping your air intake above a high waterline.

AIR INTAKE SNORKEL

The addition of a snorkel raises your air intake opening from around the level of the engine to near the roof of the vehicle. This allows for much deeper water fording and prevents the engine from sucking in water and hydro-locking. These are typically pretty pricey and reserved for serious off-road enthusiasts, but certainly worth mentioning when prepping a BOV. If you live in an area with a lot of rivers, streams, and creeks or where flooding is prone, a snorkel may be a worthy investment.

BRUSH GUARDS

A solid brush guard can protect your radiator and other front-facing engine parts when plowing through scrub brush in the median of an expressway or rubble and other urban debris on crowded city streets. They also make blasting through unsettling road blocks, fences, or gated entries less dangerous. My dad always says that it's the other people you have to worry about on the road. He's right. You can control your own vehicle, but you can't control theirs. A defensive driver is a safe driver. A brush guard is like a helmet for your vehicle. It prevents it from getting irreparable brain damage. Even a low-speed collision with another vehicle can put an immediate stop to your journey. I've seen large dogs completely incapacitate vehicles and deer can certainly do the same. You can't control that either. In a time of mass chaos, other drivers are bound to be acting and driving crazy. Consider a brush guard to

Interco Super Swampers wrapped on aluminum wheels spray painted black with standard barbecue grill paint

Rugged Ridge XHD Low/High Mount Snorkel System from the website www.ruggedridge.com

protect your vehicle's vital organs. Local welding shops and junkyards are good sources for less expensive and do-it-yourself brush guards. They

Brush guard on Ford Bronco

Brush guard on H1

may not be pretty, but remember, it's function over form.

HAND TOOLS

Let's face it. None of us should be expecting an unobstructed path of travel away from ground zero to our BOLs. The conditions will realistically be unlike anything we've ever seen or attempted to travel through before. I had a recent conversation with a guy who witnessed the chaos during Hurricane Sandy in America's Northeast. He described it as "something out of a Hollywood movie."

Bottom line, a Bug Out is anything but a *normal* trip away from home. These unusual circumstances call for a set of tools that are also unlike what we would normally pack in our vehicles. We need extreme cargo for extreme circumstances. From fences and fallen trees to locked gates and ditches, a simple hand tool can

make the difference between being stuck and moving forward. Below is a short list of tools you should consider packing in your BOV.

Gloves: Don't shred your hands unnecessarily. Buy a pair of hard-use gloves for heavy-duty tasks. I use the Reactor Hard Knuckle Gloves shown in chapter five. They are a great mix of utility, working, and tactical gloves.

Shovel: Shovels have many Bug Out uses. From shoveling snow and mud to digging fire pits and latrines, they are an incredibly versatile tool. Choose a size that best fits your vehicle. I use the US- made mud shovel from www.bullytools.com.

Wrecking/Pry Bar: A good wrecking bar is incredibly useful for prying and moving any off-road obstacle from logs to rocks. They are also a really useful urban survival tool and give incredible leverage when prying open doors, cabinets, and manhole covers or moving large chunks of concrete or building rubble.

Handsaw/Ax: I carry both. Both can make quick work of branches and small trees if blazing your own trail becomes necessary. They are also incredibly instrumental in gathering firewood. An ax is also a formidable self-defense tool.

Chainsaw: It sounds extreme, I know. But when you come up on a tree blocking a narrow stretch of road, it's the only tool that will do the job. My chainsaw is one of my last minute "throw-in" items if a Bug Out ever happens. I do not keep it in the truck all the time because an "extra" chainsaw just isn't in the budget

Bolt and Heavy Wire Cutters: Fences of some type line almost every roadway in America. The last thing I want between me and certain death is an annoying fence. Not only can bolt cutters make quick work of livestock or chain-link fences, but they can also bust open padlocks on gates (or other secure buildings, storage units, and cabinets) as well.

Tools like these can be bulky to transport and take up a lot of space. They are also unlikely to continue with you if foot travel becomes necessary. But while you're with the BOV, many off-road suppliers sell convenient mounting hardware for tools such as shovels and axes. Mounting

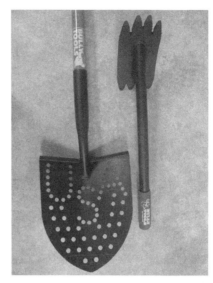

Bully Tools Mud Shovel and Wrecking Bar from www.bullytools.com

Handsaw and chainsaw for clearing brush, fallen trees, or gathering firewood

Bolt cutters

BOV HIGHLIGHT: ICON FJ45

VEHICLE MODEL: ICON FJ45
MANUFACTURER: ICON, WWW.ICON4×4.COM
PRICE: $108,000 – $220,000

ICON 4×4s certainly aren't in everyone's budget but we can all learn a lesson from these handcrafted classics. First, more is not always better. These vehicles have everything one needs to drive through the apocalypse without all the flash. They are extremely capable, yet understated in design. This is a classic BOV philosophy. Though not designed specifically with Bugging Out in mind, the tires, brush guard, off-road lights, subdued paint, and biodiesel-compatible engines sure make them outstanding BOV candidates. At the very least they are a great model for those of us building our own BOV on a budget. Clearly, ICON markets to a niche class of off-road enthusiasts but I still can appreciate the features that make these vehicles so freaking cool. Their words say it best: Hand-built bespoke utility vehicles designed to last. Vintage aesthetic, modern engineering, timeless utility.

ICON FJ45

these to a roof rack or even right on the side of your vehicle frees up important interior space for more weather-sensitive survival gear. I use the Dominion OffRoad Accessory Bars available at JeepSWAG.com, and they work perfectly.

TRACTION DEVICES

Sometimes no matter how much you dig, it's impossible to free a stuck vehicle from mud, sand, or snow. A few basic traction tools can drastically improve your chances of driving through even the worst Mother Nature has to offer.

I'm a huge fan of simplicity and fast deployment, especially in the middle of a disaster Bug Out. One of the easiest and most effective traction aids I've ever used is a product called GoTreads. They can be used with virtually any sized vehicle, even large semitrucks. They are lightweight and also fold up for easy storage. The grooved surfaces not only dig into the slippery surface (like snow or sand) but also help keep the track centered on your tire. They don't require any special tools, training, or assembly time. Just unfold, toss under your tire, and drive.

If traction devices aren't in your budget, below are a few do-it-yourself style traction options that have proven to be very effective.

Shovel and ax mounted to truck using Dominion OffRoad Accessory Bars

GoTreads traction aid in snow from gotreads.com

GoTreads in action

Kitty litter used as traction aid in slick mud

Carpet scraps repurposed for traction devices

2×4 boards arranged in washboard pattern for increased surface area

Kitty Litter: Especially in snow, kitty litter can give you the extra friction necessary to get going. Crushed oyster shells (available at most farm supply stores) also work well.

Carpet Pieces: A friend of mine packs strips of old carpet in his truck and swears by their effectiveness as a traction aid. Cut carpet in 20-inch × 3-foot (51cm × 3m) sections and place under the tire for increased friction and surface area.

Blankets: Though I've never tried this one myself, a police officer once suggested that blankets work very well as a traction aid in snow, ice, and mud.

2×4 Boards: 48-inch (4m) pieces of 2×4 boards can work wonders for getting out of a mess. Arrange them as shown in the photo to help get your tire out of mud and muck. Eight sections of 2×4 make a nice little cube for storage.

24" × 24" (61cm × 61cm) Squares of Plywood: Layers of plywood are glued together in alternating angles that make the final board incredibly strong. Plywood squares make a great traction device but also make a great base for placing a car jack in soft mud or gravel.

Even the best hand tools and traction devices may not be able to help recover a vehicle from serious jams. Sometimes, you have to call in the big boy toys.

Rugged Ridge Heavy Duty 8,500-pound (3800kg) Off Road Winch from www.ruggedridge.com

Winch pulling Creek's BOV

HOISTING, LIFTING, AND PULLING TOOLS

Winches, come-alongs, tow ropes, and chains are all valuable off-road companions. I doubt there is any serious off-road enthusiast who doesn't travel without at least one of each. Few off-road environments can stop you with these and your other hand tools.

Winch

A winch is a mechanism that allows you to pull (or even slowly let out) your vehicle. Typically, winches are electric, hydraulic, or hand-crank. If you've ever seen a tow truck pull a vehicle out of a ditch, you've probably seen a winch in action. The most popular style of off-road winches are mounted to the front or rear bumpers using a mounting plate. Winches are almost always powered by the vehicle's 12-volt electric system.

Winches contain a spool of cable or strong rope that can be attached to something solid ahead in the trail, such as a tree or another vehicle. As the winch retracts the cable, it slowly pulls your vehicle forward.

Less expensive winches can be purchased that hook onto a tow hitch in the rear. Jumper cable type leads attach to the vehicle's battery for power. This style winch is not permanently mounted and is kept inside the vehicle until needed. Having a winch option in the front and rear of a vehicle is definitely a BOV luxury. Is a winch out of your budget? Less expensive but more labor intensive options do exist.

Come-alongs and the Hi-Lift Jack

Although the Hi-Lift Jack (mentioned in chapter five) can be used to jack up your vehicle for a tire change, it can also be used as a manual hand crank winch. By first attaching the top of the Hi-Lift to your vehicle, using a chain or tow rope, and then attaching the lifting nose of the jack to a fixed object, such as a tree, you can use the Hi-Lift hand crank to slowly pull a vehicle toward the fixed object.

Come-alongs are specifically designed for this purpose. They have a cable with a hook on each end and a hand-crank ratcheting lever in the middle. As the lever is cranked, the cable retracts and helps the object "come along." At only about 10 pounds (4.5kg), come-alongs are easy to transport. They are a perfect low-cost back up winching solution for a BOV. They don't have the lifting/ pulling capacity of most electric winches, but some are rated to as much as 3 tons, or 6,000 pounds (2,700kg). That's still impressive for such a small portable tool.

Keep in mind that winches, come-alongs, and the Hi-Lift Jack can all be used to move large items out of your way as well. You may need to move a tree, broken-down vehicle, or chunk of rubble out of your path. These are multiuse tools for that as well.

Chains, Tow Straps, and Hitching Accessories

A good solid length of chain and/or tow strap can be a prepper's best friend in an off-road environment. A chain or tow strap can be used to extend the reach of your come-along, Hi-Lift jack, or electric winch. They can also be used by another vehicle to pull you out of a bad situation. A quick tow by

Hi-Lift Jack as a winching tool

Come-along in action

another vehicle is the easiest and fastest way to get out of a jam. This is one reason why I always recommend traveling in a Bug Out Convoy with other vehicles (described in chapter eight) if at all possible.

Chains are given a grade to classify them according to strength. I recommend a chain with a Grade 43 or higher for towing. Grade 70 (transport chain) is even better. It is typically a goldish color because of the chromate plating. For easy identification, chain grade should be stamped every few links with a G and then a number.

Not all tow ropes are created equal. I've had the cheap ones break just trying to pull a four-wheeler out of a ditch. Snapping a tow rope is not only frustrating, but very dangerous and could mean game over if it's your last resort. The Bubba Rope from bubbarope.com is the best tow rope I've used. The one I carry is the Renegade and has a breaking strength of 19,000 pounds (8,600kg), but they make ropes with a strength of over 130,000 pounds (59,000kg) for those of you driving monster rigs.

Many vehicles are equipped with at least one recovery hook at the front and rear for towing. I recommend including a couple of heavy-duty shackles in your off-road kit just in case. Sometimes due to an awkward angle or some other detail, a shackle is the best way to attach a tow strap, chain, winch, or come-along to a vehicle or other fixed point. My M0128 came with two shackle mounts on each bumper, which makes it easy, but in previous BOVs, I just kept my shackles in the bag with my tow rope or chain. Shackles make great tie-off points for all different types of circumstances.

Tow chain

The Renegade from www.bubbarope.com (¾" × 20' [2cm × 18m])

Recovery hook

Shackle mounted to bumpers

Shackle used as anchor point when rappelling a cliff

Additional Lighting

Disasters love to knock out electricity. Have you ever driven through a city at night when the street lamps are out? Or on a remote country road when clouds block the moon? Driving in pitch-black night can be challenging even with a good set of car headlights. Rain, snow, mud, and flying debris will only complicate your visual challenges. The addition of a few high beam aftermarket off-road lights can really help illuminate potential dangers farther ahead or even in a 360-degree radius of the vehicle (recommended). Reverse lights are almost useless in less-than-perfect conditions and a rear bumper mounted lamp can be a huge lifesaver. You must be able to *see* your threats in order to engage or avoid them. A threat can be anything from a trench of water up ahead, a nearly invisible fence, or a gang of looters hiding in the bushes. Darkness is a handicap. More lights are the solution. I mounted IPF 968 Lights to my BOV. They are not only affordable when it comes to high-quality off-road lights, but they also have a hybrid reflector that gives a combined spot and driving beam. Off-road lights aren't legal to use during normal driving on the highway, but they sure have their place in a Bug Out Scenario. It's worth noting that off-road lights may make a

IPF 968 Series Lights from www.arbusa.com

Rear bumper auxiliary lights

vehicle look "prepared." You'll have to decide if the risk is worth the reward for yourself.

SUMMARY

During Bug Out Disasters, Mother Nature is going to throw everything including the kitchen sink (literally) at you and your BOV. Floodwater, road damage, natural debris, urban debris, mudslides, severe winds, sand, snow, hail, ice, fire, lava, and everything else you can possibly imagine could be thrown in between you and your safe destination. It's important to do everything within your means to prepare for and prevent potential setbacks. The best strategy is to avoid "hot zones." Hot zone is a military term used to describe extremely dangerous areas. This may be easier said than done during a chaotic disaster. Your best defense to navigate around potential hot zones is *information*. The ability to receive and send vital information during a disaster Bug Out can be extremely instrumental in adapting your disaster plan or re-route on-the-fly based upon intelligent information. Let's discuss some options to consider when outfitting your BOV with communication and navigation tools to help you navigate through and around potential hot zones.

7 BOV COMMUNICATIONS AND NAVIGATION

IT'S NO SECRET that large disasters wreak havoc on almost every modern convenience that we've grown to know, love, and depend on in recent years. Modern technology is great until we are suddenly thrust back into a stone-age-esque way of life, even if only for a short period of time. When the grid-based services these tools depend on are ripped off-line, we must be prepared to communicate and navigate using tools that are less (or not at all) dependent on infrastructure. They must also be portable. Communication and navigation are critical components to prepping a BOV that are often underestimated or overlooked all together.

The key to all survival tools is to practice using them *before* you have to use them. This is especially true with communication and navigation tools, such as radio transceivers and global positioning systems (GPS). Some of the tools listed in this chapter can take many hours to program and/or become adequately familiar with.

This chapter has an infinite number of Bug Out implications. The ability to effectively receive information, communicate with others, and navigate during times of complete chaos is critical for a huge variety of reasons. Below are some very practical applications you may have never considered:

- communicating with family members scattered throughout a city, region, or country
- keeping up-to-date about important disaster details
- communicating with, listening to, and learning from other drivers who are also evacuating and may be many miles ahead of you
- communicating with, listening to, and learning from first responders, such as police, fire, and medical professionals
- learning of new disaster-related setbacks, such as road closures, riots, fires, or flooding
- communicating to other members of your Bug Out Team (convoy) who may be traveling in another vehicle
- communicating with your Bug Out Location about problems or estimated arrival times
- making on-the-fly disaster-related detours or trip changes

Communications tower vulnerable to disaster

BOV COMMUNICATIONS CONSIDERATIONS

Militaries and governments around the world have multiple layers of communications options in the event that one is interrupted. Certain military positions are still trained with how to communicate messages using Morse code and signal lamps. These communication layers include the most sophisticated technology in the world all the way down to a series of beeps and flashes that can be made by tapping a pipe or flashing a window on a kerosene lantern. The lesson here is that communications during times of unrest is incredibly important. There are no guarantees. We, too, should have a multilayered communications plan.

When it comes to Bug Out Communications, there are two main categories: receivers and transceivers. It's important to understand the difference. Receivers only receive information. Transceivers receive *and* transmit information. Both are excellent Bug Out resources and should be considered as pack items in your BOV. One-way communication tools only receive information. These include scanners, shortwave radios, and emergency radios. Two-way communication tools send and receive information. These include cell phones/smartphones, satellite phones, and two-way radios including walkie-talkies, Citizen Band (CB) radio, and handheld amateur (HAM) radio.

One-way Communication Tool: Scanner

Primary Function: Radio scanners are used to listen to a variety of radio frequencies including but not limited to local police, fire, commercial, airport, amateur radio, FRS/GMRS/MURS signals, CB, marine radio, and more.

Pros:

- excellent source of disaster-related information from a variety of sources
- handheld or portable units with DC car charges are excellent BOV options

Cons:

- digital versions can be expensive
- cannot transmit information, only receives information
- some models can be difficult to program and are complicated to use
- vulnerable to electromagnetic pulse

Keeping abreast of local disaster-related information is critical during a Bug Out Scenario. Traditional information sources, such as television, local radio stations, and Internet services will most certainly go off-line in a large-scale disaster. The next best source of reliable intelligence is the discussions between a variety of local radio operators.

Often referred to as a police scanner, radio scanners can actually tune into a variety of frequencies. Some of these include police, fire, AM, FM, emergency medical services, CB radio, air traffic control, marine communications, amateur radio bands, and NOAA weather broadcasts. They cannot transmit (send) information, but you can absorb an incredible amount of information by just listening. Oftentimes, the ability to receive disaster-related information is more important than being able to transmit and communicate. Scanners come in both handheld and desktop models. I'd recommend a portable handheld unit for use in a BOV.

Scanners can be manually tuned to a specific frequency. Local emergency/medical/transit frequencies can be found online at this URL: www.radioreference.com/apps/db. Local HAM radio repeaters/frequencies can be found online at this URL: www.artscipub.com/repeaters.

A printed list of these with your communication tools for the ZIP codes along your Bug Out Route is a good idea. This allows you to immediately tune into specific channels. Scanners are also designed to scan the airwaves and stop when they find an active transmission. If no one's talking, the scanner won't stop on that channel. If you don't know local frequencies, the scanner will find them,

DEFINITIONS

Power and Tower Dependence: This is the phrase I use to describe a piece of equipment that must be plugged in by cord to a power grid or that depends on a signal or service projected from a tower that is connected to the power grid.

Faraday Cage: Read chapter ten to learn how to build a Faraday cage to protect sensitive electronics, such as communications and navigation tools in the event of an electromagnetic pulse (EMP).

Faraday cage

Uniden HomePatrol portable scanner

Portable battery-powered Shortwave radio

but it may take some time to locate an active channel with active chatter. The addition of a larger external antenna helps, but isn't necessary.

In recent years, radios have become increasingly complex. This includes trunking radio systems and digital transmissions. Older scanners and many cheap models will not pick up these signals, but many small towns and other services still use the older analog systems. Digital scanners are available but as of this writing are in the five-hundred-dollar range. A digital scanner will do everything an older analog model will do plus pick up the new digital signals. One of the best units on the market is the Uniden HomePatrol. It has a built-in database of all ZIP codes in the United States and will instantly pull up available frequencies with the touch of a button. You can even update the frequencies through the Internet. It's pretty much foolproof. If you're serious about being able to scan multiple frequencies quickly and easily, you should consider this model. It's the one I have. You can use it in your home or in your BOV and it comes with a DC and AC charger for both locations. It's very simple to operate—even for a communications novice like myself. Some scanners can be difficult to use and program.

Note: Some states have restrictions on the use of scanners in vehicles. Criminals like to use radio scanners to hear the police chatter while committing a crime. Check your local laws and regulations before using a scanner in your vehicle.

One-Way Communication Tool: Shortwave Radio

Primary Function: Shortwave radios are used primarily to listen to long distance national and international radio broadcasts. However, they can also receive a variety of other transmissions including but not limited to amateur radio and transoceanic travel.

Pros:

- affordable, typically less than one hundred dollars for a decent model
- small and portable models available
- source for long distance national and international news
- can also receive some local radio transmissions

Cons:

- if new to radio communications, using a shortwave radio can take some practice
- cannot transmit information, only receives information
- vulnerable to electromagnetic pulse

Shortwave is best known for long distance broadcasting. In addition to transoceanic aircraft and vessel transmissions, AM radio and FM radio, some military communications, and commercial communications, shortwave radios can also receive shortwave programming from all over the world and are a great resource for national and international news. Many shortwave radio enthusiasts regularly listen to many different radio stations including the BBC, Radio Australia, Radio Netherlands, and many more. Thus, shortwave radio is a good source of national and global news while many of the typical grid-based systems we normally depend on are off-line. This "long distance" reception is a very unique aspect of shortwave radio bands versus many other receivers.

Shortwave radio can be tuned into a variety of frequencies, including the amateur radio bands. Make sure to purchase a radio that also receives what is referred to as *side band*. It's also often indicated as SSB on the packaging. Most amateur radio operators transmit on upper or lower side bands and your shortwave radio must have this feature in order to hear

UNDERSTANDING KHZ MHZ AND METERS

Radio bands are listed as kHZ, MHz, and METERS and are often used interchangeably. It can be really confusing! Here's how to covert between the three:

- Multiply by 1,000 to convert MHz to kHz.
- Divide by 1,000 to convert kHz to MHz.
- Divide 300 by the number of MHz to convert MHz to METERS.
- Divide 300 by the number of METERS to convert METERS to MHz.

these transmissions. Receiving FM and AM signals is pretty standard and many shortwave radios have NOAA Weather channel built in as well.

I prefer a digital shortwave radio. This allows you to tune into the exact frequency you wish, as well as store frequencies for quick access later. Analog models can be difficult to "dial in" and in my experience, reception is never as clear. Be sure to also choose a model that is battery powered so it can remain portable. An external antenna jack option is a good idea as well. Attaching a larger external antenna drastically affects reception.

This RadioShack website lists specific shortwave frequencies and is a great guide to print out and keep with your supplies: http://support.radioshack.com/support_tutorials/communications/swave-5a.htm.

One-Way Communication Tool: Emergency Radio

Primary Function: Listen to news and/or disaster-related information on AM, FM, or NOAA Weather channel.

Pros:

- very simple to use
- very affordable, less than forty dollars for a nice hand crank model
- NOAA Weather channel is a great source of disaster-related updates
- small and compact units available
- off-grid features, such as hand cranks and solar panels, are very common features
- many include other cool features, such as built-in cell phone chargers and LED flashlights

Cons:

- only receives AM, FM, and NOAA Weather channel
- cannot transmit information, only receives information
- vulnerable to electromagnetic pulse

There are many makes and models of emergency radios available. You should already have one of these in your BOB but if not, it's a must for the BOV. Many of the other communications products detailed in this chapter have the emergency radio functions already built in. The hand-crank emergency radio pictured has a built-in hand-crank cell phone charger and an LED flashlight. The hand crank can also power the radio should the batteries and built-in battery pack die. There are small emergency radios available with fewer options. In my opinion, though, the hand-crank power option is a must.

When selecting an emergency radio, it is critical to choose a model that is equipped with NOAA Weather

Hand-crank emergency radio from etoncorp.com

Charging cell phone with USB cable using hand-crank feature

Radio. Almost all modern scanners, shortwave radios, and two-way radios (discussed later) have this feature as a standard option. National Weather Radio (NWR) is a public service from the National Oceanic and Atmospheric Administration (NOAA). The NOAA broadcasts weather alerts, warnings, and disaster information twenty-four hours a day through over one thousand transmitters that cover most of the United States. Even when local radio and TV stations are not broadcasting, you should be able to get a NOAA signal. Radios must be equipped with special receivers to receive this NOAA signal and typically this station is clearly marked on emergency radios that have this feature.

In addition to weather-related information from the National Weather Service, the National Weather Radio stations can also transmit a variety of other disaster-related information by collaborating with other government entities such as FEMA and the Emergency Alert System (EAS). This can include state and local emergencies, hazards, environmental threats, and even AMBER alerts. Each state has their own EAS in place. I would suggest becoming familiar with your state's EAS policies and plans. You can find that information from the FCC at www.fcc.gov/encyclopedia/state-eas-plans-and-chairs.

Two-Way Communication Tool: Cell Phone/Smartphone

Primary function: Global private (I use that word loosely) two-way communication over cellular networks using voice, e-mail, and texting services.

Pros:
- almost everyone has a cell phone
- easy to use
- easy to power

Cell phone dropped and broken during hasty Bug Out

Cell phone GPS navigation with pre-downloaded maps

- text messaging can still be a reliable form of communication during large-scale disasters
- multifunctional (camera, variety of downloadable apps, flashlight, etc.)
- affordable
- private communication (nothing is *completely* private)
- no license required

Cons:

- completely dependent on power and tower grids
- can be affected by high call volume even when power and tower grids are not affected
- one of the first modes of communication to go off-line in a large-scale disaster
- vulnerable to electromagnetic pulse
- all activity is traceable and potentially recorded by the National Security Agency (NSA)

After Hurricane Katrina, many cell phone companies installed back-up power equipment for their cell sites and cell towers. Consequently, when Hurricane Sandy struck the East Coast and the electrical grid went down, a huge number of people in that area still had cell service. Even though backup power doesn't last forever, cellular communication has gotten a lot better during large-scale disasters in recent years. My conversations with hundreds of other disaster victims throughout the world confirm this.

However, cellular service still cannot be trusted. While the electrical issue has been addressed in many places, disasters can impact the fragile cellular network in many other ways including physical tower damage, flooding, and even high call volume. Furthermore, in the midst of a disaster Bug Out, it's not hard to imagine a cell phone getting broken or wet.

If cell towers aren't destroyed by the disaster, a cellular network can be overwhelmed by call volume. This happens quite often during disasters, large sporting events, and high-profile news events. We've all heard the message at some point in time: *Your call cannot be completed* or *all circuits are busy*. Verizon Wireless spokesman Ken Muche shed some light on this issue when interviewed by the *Los Angeles Times* in response to a 5.4 earthquake that struck Los Angeles in 2008:

"Mobile carriers project how many people will be using their phones during a crisis and try to ensure that their networks can handle that call volume, Verizon Wireless spokesman Ken Muche said. Today's call volume was 40 percent higher than what Verizon had projected for a crisis. During last year's wildfires, call volume was 600 percent higher, he said. Because of high call volume, Verizon had to start blocking some calls so that others could get through."

Knowing all of this, one would still be foolish not to bring a cell phone in the event of a Bug Out. It is an amazing tool even if the phone portion doesn't work. Below is a short list of survival-related uses for a cell phone that *is not* able to connect to a network:

- camera for taking photos or video of important information
- note pad for taking important notes
- flashlight (with flashlight app)
- survival documentation resource
- Global Positioning System (GPS) navigation

SURVIVAL QUICK TIP

If you can't get a call to go through because of high call volume, try sending a text or e-mail. Texts and e-mails require less bandwidth and signal stability than voice calls. And, both can be kept in queue for the momentary bit of signal you might need to successfully complete the transmission.

Texting may be more reliable

Two-Way Communication Tool: Satellite Phone

Primary Function: Global private (I use that word loosely) two-way communication using satellite networks.

Pros:

- long-range communication with anyone who has a working phone (landline, cell, Voice over Internet Protocol [VOIP], or satellite)
- many models can send/receive text and e-mail messages
- independent of regional power and tower grids; powered by satellite technology
- can be used even in extremely remote locations (desert, oceans)
- private communication (nothing is really private)

Cons:

- expensive (four hundred dollars plus just for the phone, not including air time or monthly charges)
- vulnerable to electromagnetic pulse

Extreme situations call for extreme communication tools. Unlike cellular and landline phones, satellite phones are typically unaffected by large-scale disasters. They don't operate on Earth-based networks like landline and cellular phones. As long as you have an unobstructed view of the sky, you'll be able to make a call from right smack dab in the center of ground zero. You can call landlines, cell phones, or satellite phones, but if the calling destination is also affected by the same disaster, they will also

TOP FREE SMARTPHONE SURVIVAL APPS

iTriage Health by iTriage LLC: Packed with great medical information

Kindle by Amazon Mobile LLC: Use this app to read books and resources stored on your phone (consider keeping survival manuals and books on your phone for easy reference during a disaster)

CoPilot Live: Excellent off-line GPS app (maps stored on phone memory card and do not require cell service to navigate)

Brightest Flashlight Free by GoldenShores Technologies LLC: Flashlight app

Scanner Radio by Gordon Edwards: Listen to police and fire scanners, weather radios, and amateur radio repeaters

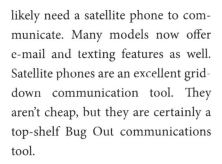

SPOT Global Phone from www.findmespot.com/GlobalPhone

Midland GXT Pro GMRS Radios from midlandusa.com

likely need a satellite phone to communicate. Many models now offer e-mail and texting features as well. Satellite phones are an excellent grid-down communication tool. They aren't cheap, but they are certainly a top-shelf Bug Out communications tool.

TWO-WAY RADIO COMMUNICATION

Radio communication is incredibly popular among members of the survival community. Many professional sectors use some form and frequency of radio communication including police and fire services, ships and marine vessels, amateur radio operators, school buses, taxi drivers, and commercial trucking operations. During large-scale disasters when most other forms of communication have failed, it is very well known and documented that radio operators are an excellent

source of disaster-related communication and information. These individuals frequently volunteer and work with first responders to weave a web of off-line communications that help to facilitate recovery. Below is a list of radio communication tools to consider for your BOV.

"Walkie-Talkies:" FRS/GMRS/MURS Radio

Primary Function: Nonprivate two-way communication over short distances. Can also listen to others who may be communicating on same channels.

Pros:

- excellent short-range patrol/convoy radios
- affordable
- new ones have multifunction features such as NOAA radio and even game calls for hunting

- no (or at least inexpensive) license required
- readily available at most outdoor retailers
- not dependent on power/tower grid
- portable and compact—easily clip them to your BOB if you leave the BOV behind

Cons:

- short range (less than one mile for FRS and five to twenty-five miles for GMRS)
- license legally required for the GMRS models
- not private
- vulnerable to electromagnetic pulse

Family Radio Service (FRS), Multi-Use Radio Service (MURS), and General Mobile Radio Service (GMRS) are very similar. These are all two-way radio walkie-talkies that you can find at most outdoor retailers. FRS is the least powerful. MURS is a step up but not by much. Neither of these two-way radios requires a license to operate, but believe it or not, the more powerful GMRS two-way radios *do* require a license from the FCC to use. It's eighty-five dollars for five years. (I wonder if all those families at Disney World I saw a few years ago got their GMRS license from the FCC before they used those walkie-talkies I saw all over the place.) You can buy GMRS radios at virtually every outdoor retail store in the world without a license, but you are supposed to get one before you use them. For many of you, I'll bet this is the first time you ever heard of that. Look at them like a fishing pole. You can buy one, but you have to have a fishing license to use it.

FRS/MURS/GMRS radios are great for short-range communications. In a grid-down scenario I suspect they will be overloaded with chatter. MURS frequencies are the

SURVIVAL QUICK TIP

Pack extra batteries! You never know when you'll need more batteries. These are much more durable than just keeping extra batteries in the packaging they come in from the store. They are cheap and an organizational wonder!

Plastic battery storage cases from www. inanycase.com

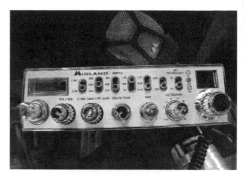

Midland xT511 Base Camp Radio with built-in NOAA Weather Radio and five power sources including Dynamo Hand Crank

Guardian Alert CB Radio from www. midlandusa.com

least popular and will probably have less traffic than the more popular FRS and GMRS models. Keep in mind the ranges quoted on the packaging are in optimal environments. Ranges in and around buildings or trees and hills are significantly shorter. However, these are ideal communications tools for a team of BOVs evacuating at the same time. As long as you have batteries (or car chargers), they will work. They are also great if a member of your Bug Out Team needs to leave the vehicle for some reason.

These are perfect patrol and scout radios. While not private, most GMRS radios have twenty-three channels and also privacy sub-channels. I've been at large sporting events with my GMRS radios and have been able to find an "almost" private channel. I say "almost" because you can never tell if someone is listening in

and just not speaking. There is absolutely no privacy with any of these radio systems.

I definitely recommend getting a nice pair of GMRS radios for your BOV. I bought an extra DC charger just in case I have to give the second unit to another vehicle. This way we can both have a radio and charger for each vehicle. I use a pair of Midland GXT Pros which have an integrated NOAA Weather Radio (discussed earlier). These have rechargeable battery packs with both a DC (cigarette lighter vehicle port) and AC charger (regular 110v plug). They are also waterproof and I've been really impressed with the range.

Citizen Band (CB) Radio

Primary Function: Nonprivate two-way communication over short distances. Can also listen to others who may be communicating on same channels. Very popular on roadways.

Pros:

- common channels for listening to updates from a variety of users in similar geographic area
- inexpensive
- decent range of up to twenty-five miles(ish)
- easy to use
- portable handheld units available
- no license required

Cons:

- not private
- dash mount units require 12V power source
- vulnerable to electromagnetic pulse

I grew up on a farm with several relatives who lived nearby. We used CB radios as a regular form of communication between homes and homes, between homes and vehicles, and between vehicles and vehicles. We could talk from home to a friend or relative in a car many miles away and often did.

CB radios are what truck drivers use, and there are forty CB radio channels. The normal range can be anywhere from one to twelve miles(ish) and depends greatly on the size of antenna, terrain, and weather. They are very popular on the roadways and operate on a different frequency than FRS and GMRS radios. Otherwise, I'd say get one or the other. For disaster preparedness, GMRS radios are excellent communication options between you and your Bug Out Team, though other people may be able to hear you if they are on the same channel. CB radios can be used the same way, but they are a better source for outside information because many users often communicate on just a couple channels. People who use CB radios typically

SURVIVAL QUICK TIP

Don't have a car charger? Consider a solar-powered charger with rechargeable batteries for charging communications tools on the go.

Solar battery charger

listen to one of two main channels: 9 (emergency channel) or 19 (traffic channel). Consequently, CB radios are great for communicating information among people in a similar geographic area. However, messages can travel long distances very fast. On the roads, truck drivers will warn other drivers on the expressway of police officers who may be hiding many, many miles ahead. The news travels fast from vehicle to vehicle and I've gotten as much as fifty miles notice before. In his book *Adrift*, Steven Callahan writes about surviving on an emergency survival dingy for seventy six days. After finally being spotted by fisherman off the coast of Marie-Galante near Guadeloupe, he writes this about his experience with CB radios:

"It seems that my parents have already heard the news. In fact, they knew of my arrival before many of the local authorities. Mathias was among the crowd when I was carried up from the beach, and he immediately sent a message on his CB radio to his friend Freddie in Guadeloupe. Freddie has an amplifier and rebroadcast the message. A man named Maurice Briand was fishing off the coast of Florida when he picked up the signal. He called my parents less than an hour after I stepped ashore. For days I won't believe that this was all possible with CB radios

External CB antenna on Creek's BOV

and not HAM units, but it turns out to be true."

I'll often flip on the CB radio when I see a traffic jam. Channel 19 is a popular channel. It never fails that the truckers from miles ahead have relayed information about the accident or event that has taken place. Then, those of us "downstream" can make decisions on the road accordingly, which typically means taking the nearest exit and mapping a detour. This is very similar to how you would use information on the CB airwaves during a disaster Bug Out.

The CB radio I use is the Guardian Alert CB Radio also made by Midland. It too has a built in NOAA Weather Band channel for instant emergency and weather updates. I chose to use a dash-mount model over a handheld unit because of the power and range, though I have both. I keep an extra handheld unit just in case I need to hand it off to another vehicle. Dash-mount CB radios do require an external antenna. These are purchased separately and are typically plug and play. These units are powered by the vehicle's electrical system and are often hardwired directly to the car battery.

Large truck stops on the freeways tend to have the best selection of CB radio units and accessories. Another great source of information and equipment is Midland USA at midlandusa.com.

Handheld Amateur Radio (HAM Radio)

Primary Function: Nonprivate global two-way communication across a network of repeaters. Can also listen to others who may be communicating on the same frequencies.

Handheld amateur radio transceivers

Pros:

- virtually unlimited in distance of communication (can even reach space)
- huge network of users (over two million worldwide)
- reliable communication network
- can develop a wide network of trusted friends in between your home and BOL who can keep you up to date on potential issues
- can listen to many radio bands including amateur radio, FRS, GMRS, police, fire, transit, airport, etc.
- can purchase mobile handheld transceivers or car mount systems and larger home units
- can own and listen without a license

Cons:

- requires license (to transmit)
- highly regulated
- most expensive of the three options for entry (licensing + equipment)
- repeater networks can fail without electricity
- home-based stations require either generator or battery power to operate during grid-down scenario
- vulnerable to electromagnetic pulse

Amateur radio (HAM radio) is considered a noncommercial recreational radio service. It fills the gap for those serious about radio communication, but it's not for commercial or public safety use. HAM radio broadcasts can be local, regional, national, and even international. A wide network of stations set up and run by amateur radio clubs and individuals makes this possible.

Using HAM radio does require a license. And, you have to pass a written test to get it. HAM operators are then assigned a call sign for legal identification. It is definitely the most powerful of the radio communication options, but also the most regulated. I am not a licensed HAM operator but am studying to take the test later this fall. I'll also be the first to admit that I am not an expert by any means on this subject. However, I do own a couple handheld HAM radio transceivers. I can't legally transmit but I can still listen, and sometimes just listening to information is the important part. You don't have to have a license to purchase an amateur radio or listen. It's amazing how much I've learned just by listening in.

HAM radio was very instrumental in helping to maintain communication among disaster relief personnel both during the September 11th terrorist attacks in New York City and Hurricane Katrina. The cool thing about HAM radio is that you can develop a network of like-minded friends—a communication network

MORSE CODE

Morse code is still very popular among HAM radio enthusiasts. In Morse code, the dots are called "dits" and the dashes are called "dahs." An internationally recognized survival emergency signal in Morse code is SOS, represented by ...---... The entire alphabet is at right.

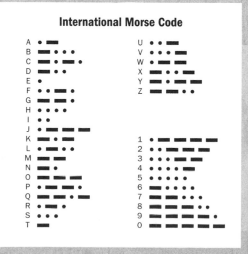

International Morse code chart

around your home and BOL and everywhere in between. Then, using a mobile HAM system during a Bug Out, you can have access to disaster-related information directly from trusted sources. Under FCC law, one must identify himself during HAM transmissions using the unique call signs. HAM radio is not private, but the call signs help to keep track of who you are communicating with when all other forms of communication are disrupted.

Repeaters allow amateur radio operators to communicate locally, but you do have to know the specific frequency to tune in. The website www.artscipub.com/repeaters has a full list of local repeaters and frequencies. Some repeaters will go down during disasters, which can have negative effects.

Many HAM radios can also be dialed in to receive many other frequencies including police, fire, public transit, medical, airport, and even raceway bands. You should print out a list of any frequencies you wish to monitor in advance. Below are websites where you can find the frequencies for your area:

- www.radioreference.com/apps/db — Fire, police, medical, and transit
- www.airnav.com/airports — airport frequencies

You may wish to familiarize yourself with police codes that are frequently used in radio transmissions. For example, 10-4 means "Message received and understood" and 11-65 means "Signal light out." A complete list of these codes can be found online at: www.radiolabs.com/police-codes.html

For more information about amateur radio, visit the National Association for Amateur Radio at www.arrl.org.

ALTERNATIVE COMMUNICATIONS AND SECRET CODES

The ability to communicate in code when traveling in a convoy (multiple vehicles evacuating together) and using public communications tools like CBs and GMRS radios is very important. As many preparedness enthusiasts often say, "Hope for the best, prepare for the worst," or "Anything that can go wrong, will go wrong." Having a pre-planned system of private code language is a great way to prepare for a worst-case scenario.

I mentioned briefly in *Build the Perfect Bug Out Bag* that myself and the other members of my Bug Out convoy each carry a code card. This is a card that lists different "FLASH" codes for a variety of commands and/or responses. We can communicate basic codes to one another using flashlights or beeps from our GMRS two-way radios should the need arise for "secret" communication. It's our own private version of Morse code. I keep a code card attached to the back of the sun visor on my BOV as well as in my Bug Out Bag.

A similar concept is to develop communication code words for popular phrases you might use to communicate with your convoy during a Bug Out. These could be used to communicate under the radar if you know others are listening. Below is a list of ideas to get you thinking:

- Alpha = lead vehicle
- Bravo = second vehicle in line
- Charlie = third vehicle in line
- Honey Hole = bathroom break
- Mr. Jones = potential human threat
- Whoopie = need to refuel
- Larry = left
- Roger = right

- High Tide = switch to backup radio frequency, main channel compromised

Private code systems not only provide a crude backup form of offline communication but are also really fun to practice with your family and other members of your Bug Out Team. Before too long, you'll have your own coded language with a little practice.

BOV NAVIGATION CONSIDERATIONS

Navigating by the sun, moon, and stars is fine and well if you are Lewis and Clark and don't have to mitigate through and around roads, cities, fences, buildings, bridges, and concrete jungles. Modern society presents a vast myriad of hurdles to navigate, and it is extremely difficult (if not impossible) to travel without a digital or paper map. Let's explore your BOV navigation options.

CLOCK DIAL DIRECTIONS

Use the hours of an imaginary clock face to communicate directional coordinates to other members of your Bug Out Team. For example, "Watch out, fallen tree at 2 o'clock." This method is very quick and easy to communicate. It's also easy to understand. Short, sweet, and to the point.

X
YOU ARE HERE

Dog at 11 o'clock and car at 3 o'clock

Window-mount GPS unit and cell phone GPS using RAM X-Grip from www.rammount.com

Handheld backcountry GPS unit

Global Positioning System (GPS) Unit

Primary Function: Satellite-based stand-alone navigation tool used to navigate roadway and backcountry travel. Can also be used to log travel and store trips.

Pros:

- unaffected by power and tower grids
- very accurate when out in the open
- easily powered with 12V vehicle system or batteries
- the handheld backcountry units are often shock resistant and water-proof

Cons:

- go "out of service" when blocked by trees, buildings, and other obstructions
- some are not waterproof
- vulnerable to electromagnetic pulse

- not always up-to-date with most current maps

Portable GPS units have come a long way in recent years. From handheld, portable backcountry units to ones designed for vehicles, they are quickly replacing the paper maps people used to depend on for travel. Contrary to popular belief, GPS units are not affected by most large-scale regional disasters. They will still work as long as they have power. In a wide-scale global disaster, this is obviously not the case. GPS units communicate with low-atmosphere satellites that are unaffected by power and tower grids. These are excellent BOV navigation tools to make quick route changes and detours.

Smartphone-Based GPS

Primary Function: Smartphone-based navigation tool for traveling and navigating roadways and backcountry (very limited in most cases without special downloaded apps). Cell phone service and/or off-line downloaded maps are typically necessary to use this function when power and tower grids are affected.

Pros:

- stand-alone GPS function is possible, but finicky
- do not need another electronic piece of equipment, GPS built into cell phone
- does not require cell service, if planned in advance (only applicable to some models)

Cons:

- drains battery quickly
- must have app and off-line maps loaded in advance of disaster
- not all phones are created equal, some work and some do not
- signal affected by buildings, trees, and terrain
- not as robust as stand-alone GPS unit

Most smartphones are now equipped with GPS chips and software. Like stand-alone GPS units, many smartphones (not all) can provide off-line navigation that is independent of cell phone service. Most smartphones use what is called assisted GPS or aGPS. This means that the phone uses the cellular connection to "assist" with the GPS data provided by the satellites. This process provides for quicker connection and navigation functions. However, assisted GPS only works when the phone has reliable cell service, which is not likely during a disaster. Many navigation apps (like Google Maps) also depend on a reliable data connection and will not function off-line. However, there are certain apps you can download that also include off-line maps. As long as your phone is GPS capable and you have a navigation app capable of using off-line maps stored on your phone's memory card, you should be able to use your smartphone as a stand-alone GPS without a cellular data connection. You *must* try this in advance to make sure it works on your phone! I have a Motorola Droid and can do this using the CoPilot Live app that I downloaded for free. Keep in mind that the GPS capabilities of smartphones aren't yet as robust as a stand-alone unit, so it will often take a smartphone longer to pinpoint an initial location. Mine takes as much as ten minutes sometimes. And, it is a major battery drain.

A nice dash- or window-mounting system makes using a cell phone for navigation or communication much easier and safer while driving. In a chaotic Bug Out, having your

Paper atlas and magnetic compass

12V cigarette-lighter-style power port

DC/AC inverter

cell phone easily accessible is a must. I've found that the best smartphone mount for bumpy rides is the RAM X-Grip from rammount.com.

Paper Map and Compass

Electronics come with no guarantee. They are all susceptible to many potential setbacks. No matter what electronic navigation tools you've chosen to include in your BOV, you should also include a paper map and traditional magnetic compass. Neither is power and tower dependent. Even though I carry a paper map and compass in my Bug Out Bag, I also have an atlas and window-mount compass in my BOV. I like the idea of keeping my Bug Out Bag intact and not having its contents spread throughout the truck. Just like the map in my BOB, my paper atlas is marked with three different routes to my BOL for easy reference.

POWERING ELECTRONICS IN A BOV

It's important to make a quick note about powering your BOV communications and navigation tools. Almost all of the items we've discussed can be powered through a 12V cigarette lighter connection, batteries, or direct hardwire to the vehicle's battery. It's important to make sure you have these chargers/cables/batteries already packed in your vehicle.

If car chargers are lost or not available, affordable DC/AC inverters can be purchased at almost any retailer that sells automotive supplies. Inverters plug into any DC power port (cigarette lighter) and convert DC power (power from your car battery) to AC power (like in your house). This allows you to plug standard 110V plugs into the inverter. These can be chargers for even larger items, like laptops and radios.

Should you have to abandon the vehicle and continue on foot, you'll have to decide what, if any, of these electronics will continue on the journey. Mobile power options, such as solar chargers or extra batteries, will need to be considered to power most of them on foot.

SUMMARY

The key elements in putting together a good BOV communications and navigation system are as follows:

- You should have at least one communications and navigation option that *is not* power and tower dependent.
- You should have at least one battery-powered receiver to receive disaster-related information in the event traditional news channels are not operating.

- All tools should be practiced and easy to use, even under stress.
- You need to have a way to power (and recharge) your electronic tools.
- All tools need to be installed and ready to use in your BOV.
- You should have at least one backup form of two-way communications to cell phones (GMRS radios are first choice and CB radio is second choice).
- Communications channels for FRS/GMRS/CB/HAM radio should be chosen in advance and all members of the Bug Out Team should know what these channels are for each device.

My first three purchases in the communications department were an SSB-capable shortwave radio receiver (TECSUN PL-660), a pair of GMRS two-way radios (Midland) (license required) with integrated NOAA Weather Band, and a dash-mounted CB radio (Midland). I later purchased a digital scanner (Uniden HomePatrol) and a handheld amateur radio transceiver (Baofeng) to receive a variety of local emergency services transmissions along a Bug Out Journey. I am still very much a novice with amateur radio.

8 VEHICLE SECURITY AND DEFENSE

NOTHING UP TO THIS POINT MATTERS if you can't protect yourself, your family, and your survival supplies should the need arise.

Theft, looting, rape, violent crime, and even murder are very common during chaotic large-scale disasters. In fact, they are so common that entire organizations exist to help victims of violent crime during disasters. It's a well-known fact among law enforcement personnel that criminals look forward to the cloak of darkness and chaos that a disaster presents. Some criminals even travel hundreds of miles to disaster areas to take advantage of the opportunity. If you abandon your home during a Bug Out, you can fully expect that looters who risk life and limb to stay behind will go through it. Allow me to pull a section called "The Ugly Truth" from my first book, *Build the Perfect Bug Out Bag*.

THE UGLY TRUTH

Disasters have devastating consequences and can leave people, cities, and regions with horrific and unimaginable circumstances. I am always amazed at how generous my fellow Americans are when responding to help victims of disaster. It seems that disaster sometimes brings out the absolute best in people. Whether it be in the form of donations or hands-on labor, it is very moving to see people rally behind those who have suffered so much loss. These efforts are always covered by news outlets weeks and months after a disaster strikes.

Unfortunately, however, there are people in this world who do not share the same sentiment for our hurting brothers and sisters. For some, disasters bring out their worst qualities. These predators use the chaos and disorder that surround disasters to further victimize people through looting, robbing, violence, and rape. These events are rarely, if ever, mentioned by news outlets—leaving many unaware of the potential dangers. This reality is the darkest side in any disaster situation and is rooted in selfishness, greed, and sometimes desperation.

It's no mystery that large-scale disasters overwhelm normal public-safety operations—at least temporarily. It's during this time when most violent crimes occur. You must be prepared to defend you and your family from individuals and gangs should the need arise. Whether you like the idea or not, you would be naïve and foolish not to take this category seriously—especially if traveling with women and small children.

BOV SELF-OFFENSE

The best form of self-defense is avoiding contact to begin with. The fewer people you encounter the better. Get out of the city and away from people as fast as possible and stay out. Stick to less traveled back roads rather than expressways. Every time you stop, there is increased risk. Don't stop for anyone or anything unless absolutely necessary. I don't even like the idea of stopping at official roadblocks because "official" can easily be faked and I don't trust many "officials" to begin with. I will certainly try to detour around those if possible. I don't want anyone getting in the way of where I'm headed.

Before we get into a discussion about BOV defense tools and weapons, there are a few basic security strategies to consider:

Convoy

When possible, travel with other vehicles. There is power in numbers and an entire convoy of vehicles is much less likely to be compromised than just one traveling alone. You can share resources and intelligence.

Know Your Routes

Know your primary and two back-up routes by heart. You should know the vulnerabilities and strengths of each route, such as choke points (like bridges), flood-prone areas, cliffs, buildings, water sources, etc. The more you know about your route the better prepared you are to deal with potential and unexpected events along the way.

Duty Assignments

Ideally, each BOV has a dedicated team member for driving, navigation/security, and communications. Any extra members should be on the lookout for potential threats including road damage, hot spots of rioting or violence, or other dangers. It's nearly impossible for the driver to also manage security and navigation during times of stress, such as avoiding dangerous roadblocks or steering clear of aggressive evacuees. Map reading and navigation during a sudden detour can be a full-time job.

ESCAPE, EVASION, SURVEILLANCE, AND FAIR WARNING

BOV security and self-defense isn't restricted to just self-defense weapons. As I mentioned earlier, the best form of self-defense is avoiding conflict altogether. Surveilling ahead, setting perimeter alarms, and camouflaging are all offensive measures to prevent surprise encounters.

BOV Perimeter Alarms

Setting a perimeter alarm around camp during an unexpected overnight stay on a Bug Out Journey can serve as an extra set of "eyes and ears" for potential threats.

Motion Sensor Driveway Alarms:
Motion sensor driveway alarms make excellent perimeter alarms. They are inexpensive and easy to deploy. Many of them have a range of several hundred feet and even operate on battery and DC power, which is perfect for a mobile setup. If you go this route, get one with both silent and audible notification options. You may not want the audible alarm to sound for the sake of discretion.

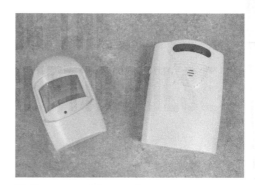

Motion sensor driveway alarm

Pull-String Firecrackers: Cheap pull-string firecrackers make great quick and dirty perimeter alarms. Fasten a trip line to one side and the other side to a stake or tree. The firecracker pops when the trip line is triggered. The trick to setting these is to make your trip line very tight so that the slightest tug sets it off.

Cheap pull-string firecrackers and a spool of military surplus tripwire

12-Gauge Blank Perimeter Alarm: This nifty perimeter alarm fires off a blank 12-gauge shotgun shell when tripped. Typically, it's just the primer that fires, but even that is plenty loud. It's reusable with extra 12-gauge blanks and is perfect for scaring the pants off would-be intruders or even large wild game, such as bear and wolves. This alarm can be heard for many yards away.

DIY Rat Trap Alarm: Not only are rat traps excellent small game food trapping tools, but they can also serve as dual-purpose perimeter alarms. Drill

12-gauge perimeter alarm from www.pyrocreations.com

DIY rat trap perimeter alarm

Binoculars

a hole in the base and screw it to a tree or doorjamb. Then set the trap and attach your trip wire to the trigger lever. The loud snap from a rat trap can be heard for several hundred feet, even in dense woods or in abandoned homes. The hole in the base can also be used to secure the trap with Paracord to a fixed object when used for trapping small game. Rat traps are excellent tools for trapping squirrel and chipmunk.

BOV Surveillance

Binoculars: Binoculars are perfect for avoiding potential messes ahead. From positively identifying uniformed personnel to verifying road damage, the ability to see far into the distance is a huge advantage. A good rifle scope can serve double duty for this use as well.

I have a pair of Bushnell 7×50 binoculars in my BOV that I received as a gift a long time ago. They are waterproof and perfect for my needs.

Bushnell makes several 7×50 and 7×35 models that are under one hundred dollars. Binoculars are labeled with two numbers: The first is the level of magnification, and the second is the diameter of the front lenses (the ones farthest from your eyes). For example, 7×35 binoculars are smaller than 7×50 binoculars. Larger lenses will let in more light but are also bulkier for mobile travel like in a Bug Out Bag. Also, 10×50 binoculars are more powerful than 7×50 binoculars. The object will appear 10 times closer than with the naked eye with 10×50s versus 7 times closer with 7×50s.

Night Vision: It's not hard for me to imagine a circumstance when I might want to survey my immediate area at night without using a "beacon in the night here I am" flashlight. Night vision goggles, scopes, binoculars, and monoculars offer a huge tactical advantage when attempting to mitigate nighttime threats.

Creek in head-mounted night vision goggles

Waterproof WayPoint light from www.streamlight.com

Night vision optics that also magnify are really expensive. Some great Bushnell Gen 1 Night Vision Monoculars can be found on Amazon.com for less than two hundred dollars. These are entry-level monoculars but will still get the job done. Other affordable brands are Yukon and Night Owl.

Spot Light: Whether changing a tire in the middle of the night or assessing off-road angles out of your BOV headlamp range, a mobile spotlight certainly has its advantages. My WayPoint from streamlight.com is rechargeable and came with a convenient mounting bracket. Sometimes you just need a high-power mobile spotlight to light up the night sky.

BOV Camouflage

As I say to my students at Willow Haven, "The guy in the worst predicament is the guy who has no options." The ability to camouflage your BOV gives you options. What if you have to scout on foot away from the BOV for an alternative path to travel? What if you have to pull off the road to camp or take a break? What if you have to abandon your BOV in a small patch of woods, but you plan to come back for it later? BOV camouflage may be the one thing that saves your BOV from getting ransacked and looted. It can also prevent would-be threats from seeing you while passing through the vicinity.

I pack a 10' × 20' (3m × 6m) military-style woodland camo netting tarp from camonettingstore.com. This is a quick and easy way to make my BOV virtually disappear in plain sight when near or in a forest setting. It can also be used to cover a gear stash or even camouflage a camp area if necessary.

Natural camouflage can also be deployed in a pinch. At Willow Haven, I teach how to naturally

10' × 20' camo netting from www.camonettingstore.com draped over an SUV

Natural camo on Creek's hand: Mud layer

Natural camo on Creek's hand: Debris layer

camouflage your body and the technique is equally effective when working with vehicles. The concept starts with mud. Slather on a nice wet and gooey layer of mud that can be found in most ditches and riverbanks. Next, grab fistfuls of debris from the forest floor and smash it on the mud. The leaves, grasses, twigs, and pieces of bark will stick to the mud and provide the most realistic looking break-up camo pattern you've ever seen.

Abandoning Your BOV

Camouflage isn't the only tactic you can use to protect an abandoned BOV until recovery is possible. If it comes to that, you must understand that everything left behind is as good as gone. If you can't take your supplies with you or cache them in a safe place, they will likely be stolen by looters or destroyed by the disaster that threatens you.

Regardless, if you have to abandon, there are a few tactics you can use to increase your chances of at least salvaging the vehicle.

Hide the Battery: Use the tools in your vehicle maintenance kit to remove the car battery and hide it nearby. This would drastically affect a thief's ability to steal your BOV.

Locking Gas Cap: While not a guarantee against theft, potential fuel looters will quickly move to vehicles that do not have locking gas caps to source fuel.

Steering Wheel Lock: You can purchase a steering wheel lock or do what the military does and weld two chains to the floorboard that padlock around the steering wheel.

BOV WEAPONS

Like the scenarios described in the beginning of this chapter, sometimes you can do everything right and still be faced with difficult decisions. You are only one-half of the self-defense equation. A violent attacker may give you no choice but to use some type of force protection—lethal or nonlethal. Let's discuss some viable BOV weapons. Keep in mind that any weapon can be forcibly taken and used against you as well.

BOV NONLETHAL WEAPONS

The decision to take someone's life should be an absolute last resort. It's not hard at all to imagine the need to deter potential attackers rather than kill them. Nonlethal weapons are perfect for these types of scenarios.

Pepper Spray

There is a reason why military, police, and security professionals carry pepper spray—it works! I have a Tornado brand dash-mount pepper spray in my BOV. No matter what brand you

Naturally camouflaged front fender of a vehicle

Welded chain steering wheel lock

Tornado brand pepper spray in convenient cigarette lighter vehicle mount from www.gettornado.com

choose, you want your BOV pepper spray to be easy to access and deploy. You may only be given a few seconds to react and you don't want to be fumbling through the glove box or center console when every second counts. Gettornado.com has a few great vehicle-mounted pepper spray options.

If you already have a bottle of pepper spray, double-sided Velcro makes an excellent makeshift mounting system. Simply wrap the bottle with an adhesive-backed hook or loop and then screw a strip of the opposite side against your dash for a secure mount. I've found that if you just apply the Velcro to the dash with an adhesive backing it will come loose in extreme heat.

A pepper spray jogger armband can also be repurposed to wrap around the sun visor for quick and easy overhead access.

Below are my general guidelines when it comes to purchasing and using pepper spray:

Oleoresin Capsicum: Buy a pepper spray that has the active ingredient oleoresin capsicum. Oleoresin capsicum is derived from pepper plants and is extremely effective in irritating the eyes, airways, and lungs of an attacker. The spray you choose should have around 5 to 8 percent oleoresin capsicum. Tornado brand has 10 percent. A pepper

Tornado brand surface mounted pepper spray in Creek's BOV

Makeshift Velcro pepper spray mount

Maglite LED D-Cell mounted to vehicle pillar

spray's strength is measured by Scoville Heat Units (SHU). Anything in 2,000,000 SHU range is sufficient.

Spray and Retreat! Don't hang around to watch what happens. The entire purpose of pepper spray is to disorient and demobilize an attacker long enough for you to escape. Spray your attacker and after you confirm a direct hit, retreat immediately. Any decent pepper spray should buy you enough time to get away safely.

Know the Local Laws: Pepper spray is legal in all fifty states, but some states have imposed certain restrictions. Be sure to check your local and state laws to see if they have any that apply specifically to the purchase and use of pepper spray.

MELEE AND IMPACT BOV WEAPONS

Almost anything that can be swung, thrust, or thrown at an attacker can fit into this category. There are a few items, however, that are worth considering specifically.

Maglite LED D-Cell

Not only are Maglite's LED D-Cell iconic lighting tools popularized by the law enforcement community, but they also make very efficient impact weapons. The machined aluminum construction weighted by chunky D-cell batteries carries quite the punch when swung in self-defense. The

Crovel multiuse survival and self-defense tool from www.gearupcenter.com

waterproof flashlight is just a bonus. Handy mounting clips are available for mounting these "flashlights" within easy reach.

Crovel

GearUp's Crovel is an excellent multiuse survival tool and can easily serve double duty as a wicked self defense weapon. From the hooked hammerhead pry bar to the sharpened shovel edge, I wouldn't ever want to be downrange of this tool. You can dig a latrine and protect your family all with one tool.

Telescopic Batons

Popularized by Armament Systems and Procedures Inc., telescoping batons are often referred to as an ASP. This style of baton is quickly replacing the wooden versions. Telescopic batons are used primarily by the security and law enforcement sectors as a nonlethal tool for controlling unruly subjects. They are ideal for strategic strikes to the body or for choking and body restraints. Contact ASP online at www.asp-usa.com for certified training instructors in your area.

MISCELLANEOUS WEAPONS

I'd love to detail every potential BOV weapon available, but the list is longer than space allows. From knives and machetes to homemade clubs and tomahawks, the possibilities are endless. The photo includes several other weapons to get you thinking.

BOV GUNS

While nonlethal self-defense tools are great options to broaden your overall BOV security plan, guns are my first option for self-defense. It is my opinion that you should not pack guns in your BOV that you cannot also carry if you have to abandon your BOV. Others may disagree. The last thing you want is to leave one of your guns behind or have to stash it because it's too heavy to keep carrying. The only exception is if you install some kind of gun safe in your BOV and, even then, it's questionable.

Bug Out Guns is probably the most heavily debated topic among survival enthusiasts. Literally everyone has a different opinion about what and what not to take. And,

Telescopic baton extended

Potential BOV weapons

Creek's .357 Magnum Bug Out Bag gun

quite frankly, there are many valid variations. Firearms are very personal tools and consequently most people have different thoughts when it comes to Bug Out Guns. The following are simply my thoughts on the subject, and I hope they help you to choose a combination of guns and ammunition that you are happy with.

As I detail in *Build the Perfect Bug Out Bag*, I carry a handgun (.357 revolver) in my Bug Out Bag. I believe all permit-holding and trained adults should carry a handgun. If I were to Bug Out on foot from the start, I would take this one gun because of weight and keeping a low profile. However, if evacuating by BOV, I will definitely be taking a long gun and another pistol of a different type. I have chosen a long gun that I can take with

me and conceal if I have to abandon the truck. I'll discuss this later.

Below are five basic categories of guns that I think everyone should consider when preparing a BOV for disaster. I list what I believe to be the pros and cons of each. There is no perfect gun for any given situation. No matter what you choose there will be compromise.

Revolvers

As I've already stated, I choose to carry a .357 revolver in my BOB for self-defense. I've fired thousands of rounds downrange with about every type of handgun you can imagine and I've never had a revolver fail me. I can't count the number of times I've have semiautomatic pistols jam or fail. Even the split second

SURVIVAL QUICK TIP

Being chased by a bad guy? Consider packing caltrops. Caltrops are a medieval antipersonnel devices made from metal spikes situated in such a way that, when thrown on the ground, land with a spike pointing up every time. These can be homemade by welding thick four- to five-inch nails in the center and bending them in such a way that a point always points upward. The nail heads need to be ground down to points as well.

Homemade nail caltrops (left) and store-bought caltrops (right)

Revolver cylinder

Creek's Glock 19 semiautomatic pistol

it takes to clear a jam counts. When it comes down to pulling the trigger for self-defense, I want a revolver in my hand. Don't consider any caliber smaller than a 9mm for self-defense. I love to shoot .22 caliber pistols but I don't want one for self defense. Choose a larger round with knock-down power. My philosophy with self-defense is that you don't shoot to injure, you shoot to kill. If someone or something (bear, dog, zoo animal) has pushed you to the point of drawing your gun and pulling the trigger, you want the result to bring finality to the situation. But, as many of you semiautomatic lovers are already saying to yourselves, there are drawbacks to revolvers. Below is an unbiased evaluation.

Pros:

- incredibly reliable (I have never in my life had one jam or fail to fire.)
- easy to reload
- easy to operate; no levers, buttons, magazine releases, etc.
- few moving/working parts

Cons:

- very limited bullet capacity, typically six rounds
- normally bulkier and heavier than most semiautomatic handguns
- takes longer to reload versus dropping and slamming in another magazine
- no safety (not necessarily a con but worth mentioning)

Semiautomatic Pistols

Now don't get me wrong, I love my semiautomatic pistols and I'd be thrilled to have any of them in a Bug Out Scenario. In fact, I installed an under-dash-mounted holster from Texas Custom Holsters in my BOV for my 9mm Glock 19 just in case I

Under-dash-mounted holster from www.texascustomholsters.com

Creek's Mossberg 500 mounted to roof of BOV using a rack from www.bigskyracks.com

decide to bring it along. This is also one of my everyday carry guns, and when I drive the BOV, I transfer it from my concealed carry holster to the dash holster for quick access. Semiautomatic handguns certainly have their advantages, but they aren't perfect.

Pros:

- larger bullet capacity: Most factory magazines are at least ten and high-capacity magazines can be purchased for many models that extend that to as high as thirty rounds. My Glock came with fifteen round mags. Check your local laws and regulations.
- typically lighter weight than revolvers, especially polymer built models
- typically more slim-line and less bulky, easier to conceal

- faster to reload: The press of a button ejects the spent magazine and a fresh one can instantly be replaced.
- customizable with aftermarket grips and accessories, such as lasers and lights

Cons:

- they do jam
- require more skill to operate, troubleshoot, and clean
- more moving parts, such as slides, levers, buttons
- typically more expensive than revolvers

Pump 12-Gauge Shotguns: Mossberg 500 or Remington 870

These shotguns are two of the most versatile firearms ever made. Both the 500 and 870 are highly customizable with aftermarket grips, stocks, butt pads, and accessories. Both are used extensively by police and military personnel. I own a Mossberg 500 but it's really a personal choice between the two guns. You can't go wrong either way.

Twelve-gauge shotguns are outstanding self-defense guns. Just the sound of racking a shell into the chamber is a deterrent in and of itself. There are basically three types of ammunition for a shotgun; bird shot, 00-buck, and slugs. Bird shot is for hunting birds and small game. 00-buck and slugs are designed for hunting larger game. 00-buck is also the round of choice for self-defense. Not only is 00-buck like firing ten 9mm bullets at one time, but as these balls travel, they also spread out. It's safe to say that you might be a little nervous if ever in a close quarter self-defense scenario. The spread pattern of 00-buck helps to make up for your less-than-perfect aim. Chances are it will be lights out as long as you're pointing in the general direction of the target.

Shotguns are amazing hunting weapons. From dove and quail to deer and wild boar, you can effectively hunt almost any animal on the planet with a 12-gauge shotgun. The 500 and 870 are also fairly easy to troubleshoot and clean in the field with basic tools (previous practice required). The pistol grip option converts the gun into a much more packable Bug Out Weapon for urban, up-close environments. It's possible, but certainly not ideal, to hunt with a pistol grip shotgun. State regulations about shotguns with pistol grips vary. Check your state laws about restrictions on hunting and traveling with a shotgun outfitted with a pistol grip. Federal and state laws apply before, during, and after a large-scale Bug Out Scenario.

I keep a Mossberg 500 at home for self-defense and at my BOL for self-defense, but I do not plan to pack one in my BOV. I just prefer to travel lighter and more low profile if I have to walk, but many do not share these preferences.

Pros:

- highly customizable
- versatile hunting and self-defense weapons
- powerful knockdown power
- field tested for many years by military and police professionals
- affordable—three hundred to five hundred dollars and even less used

Cons:

- hard to conceal if traveling by foot
- heavy to transport

AR-15

The AR-15 rifle is the semiautomatic civilian version of the M16 military

Stock of Mossberg 500 fitted with compact survival kit

AR-15 with a stack of extra magazines

rifle. Colt was the first to offer this style of rifle to civilians in the 1960s. Now, however, there are many variants sold by many different manufacturers and they are all generally referred to as AR-15s. This is an awesome rifle that can be configured to take a variety of ammunition calibers. .223 is a very popular AR-15 caliber.

The AR-15 rifle one of the best-selling platforms ever produced. Literally hundreds, maybe even thousands, of aftermarket accessories are available. ARs are excellent varmint and large game hunting guns but they excel in the arena of self-defense. After all, it is a finely tuned descendent of similar arms carried by soldiers in combat. It has excellent long-range defensive capabilities but is flexible enough to be very effective in close quarters as well with collapsible stocks and shorter barrel lengths. Most people buy ARs because they are inarguably one of the best self-defense guns available to mankind and have a high-capacity magazine. Whether defending your BOV or your BOL against enemies domestic or foreign, an AR-15 offers you the reliability, the power, the design, the accuracy, and the reputation to get the job done right. With all of that said, I keep an AR at my BOL, but not in my BOV. I have many acquaintances that pack ARs in their BOVs. If you have to walk, it's hard to conceal an AR-15. Like with the shotguns, I prefer to travel lighter with a low profile if I'm forced to Bug Out on foot.

Pros:

- highly versatile with countless aftermarket accessories
- powerful calibers
- effective in close quarters and at great distances
- very accurate
- easy to operate
- low recoil
- lightweight as far as rifles go

Henry AR-7 disassembled with barrel stowed in stock for easy transport

Henry AR-7 in action

- high-capacity magazine (from ten to one hundred rounds)
- quick and easy to change magazines
- excellent for hunting and self-defense

Cons:

- not compact for low profile foot travel or concealed carry
- too much gun for small game hunting
- expensive (especially when politics get involved)
- ammunition is expensive and at the time of this writing, very difficult to even find
- strict(er) regulations and limitations for ownership in some areas

.22 Caliber Rifle (Creek's BOV Long Gun)

While .22 rifles don't have the tactical advantages of a shotgun or AR-15,

they are amazing weapons nonetheless. I have chosen to pack the Henry U.S. Survival AR-7 in my BOV. When it comes to .22s, there are many models from many manufacturers to choose from. I prefer a takedown model, which breaks down into more packable and concealable sections. The Henry U.S. Survival AR-7 does this as does the Ruger 10/22 Takedown. At 3.5 pounds (1.6kg), the AR-7 is my Bug Out Long Gun of choice.

Most .22 rifles are notoriously accurate and they make excellent all-around survival guns. The guns and ammunition are both very affordable and accessible. This caliber is also not highly regulated, unlike many of the more powerful rifles. They are also lighter and less bulky than other larger guns. The one big disadvantage is that the .22 caliber bullet is not a powerful takedown round—for hunting or self-defense. However, I have

BOV GUN HIGHLIGHT: U.S. SURVIVAL AR-7

GUN MODEL: AR-7

MANUFACTURER: HENRY REPEATING ARMS, HENRYREPEATING.COM/RIFLE-SURVIVAL-AR7.CFM

CALIBER: .22 LONG RIFLE

CAPACITY: EIGHT-ROUND MAGAZINE (COMES WITH TWO)

WEIGHT: 3.5 POUNDS (1.6 KG)

LENGTH: 16.5 INCHES (42CM) WHEN STOWED, 35 INCHES (89CM) WHEN ASSEMBLED

PRICE: MSRP $280

The AR-7 rifle was designed with survival in mind. In fact, the AR-7 has been the survival rifle of choice for the U.S. Air Force since 1959. It is an amazing small game hunter for gathering food off the grid but can also serve as an emergency backup self-defense gun if necessary. I wouldn't want to be sniped in the head, chest, neck or face by a .22 rifle, would you?

As if those qualities aren't good enough, the AR-7 does something that no other rifle on the market can: The barrel and receiver detach and fit into the impact-resistant and water-resistant molded stock. Once packed, it can be easily stowed out of sight in a backpack, canoe, or under a seat. The unique casing keeps it protected even in the harshest disaster conditions.

It comes with two eight-round magazines. You can easily pack hundreds of .22 long rifle bullets in a BOV or BOB. .22 caliber rounds are smaller and lighter as compared to shotgun and AR rounds and are much easier to transport.

Henry AR-7

put more food on the table with my .22 than any other gun I own. I have also heard firsthand accounts of people taking game as large as wild boar and deer with very selective head shots. And I don't know about you, but I sure wouldn't want to get shot in the face with a .22 rifle.

If you choose to pack a .22 rifle, other members of your Bug Out Team could also add .22 LR pistols to their kit and you could share ammo. Most of these models are small and lightweight. They aren't the first choice for self-defense guns, but they make a great backup.

Pros:

- takedown versions are lightweight and very packable
- affordable guns
- affordable ammunition
- ammunition is small and lightweight
- excellent small game hunters and sniping rifles

Cons:

- not best choice for self-defense
- non-takedown models can be bulky and hard to conceal
- at the time of this writing, ammunition is very difficult to even find

SELF-DEFENSE TRAINING COURSE HIGHLIGHT

COURSE NAME: MAG 40
WEBSITE: MASSADAYOOBGROUP.COM
INSTRUCTOR: MASSAD AYOOB

This is an intense, four-day, forty-hour immersion course in the "rules of engagement" for armed, law-abiding private citizens. The course emphasizes legal issues, tactical issues, and aftermath management. Topics will include interacting with suspects, witnesses, responding police officers, threat recognition, and mind-set, and the management of the social and psychological aftermath of having to use lethal force in defense of self or others. Also covered is preparing beforehand for legal repercussions and minimizing your exposure to them. Situations in the home, at the place of business, or "on the street" will all be covered. Range work will include instruction in the use of the defensive handgun under extreme stress. Drawing from concealment, two-handed stances, shooting from cover, one-handed stances with either hand, speed reloading, and more are taught with an overall emphasis on fast, accurate shot placement. The course will culminate with a written examination covering the classroom topics and a police-style handgun qualification course.

DEFENDING YOUR EGO VERSUS DEFENDING YOUR BODY

I'm the first to admit that I am not an expert when it comes to the legal nuances of self-defense. Quite frankly, it can be a really confusing subject based on mixed accounts of what really happened. I do know two things. First, you can only act in self-defense if you feel threatened with physical injury or death. I take that to mean my loved ones as well. You can only defend threats to your physical body, not your pride or ego. There is a huge difference. Second, you need to take the phrase "anything you say can and will be used against you in a court of law" really seriously. That means you don't say anything to anyone without a trusted attorney present. Sometimes it seems the law favors the attacker more than those defending themselves, and just a few ill-chosen words can change the course of your life even if your actions were completely legal. The laws of our country exist before, during, and after a Bug Out Scenario.

How and when you will use self-defense tools and tactics to keep you and your loved ones safe is a very personal decision with very serious ramifications. Self-defense is serious business and further reading on the subject is highly recommended. Look for firearm and lethal use of force training courses that may be offered in your area.

SUMMARY

The United States military has a training program titled SERE, which stands for Survival, Evasion, Resistance, and Escape. This program, among other things, helps prepare and equip (mentally and physically) soldiers who may find themselves behind enemy lines in the line of duty. Large-scale disasters that warrant a full-scale Bug Out can create circumstances that may feel like a war zone, complete with obstacles, chaos, and even combative attackers. You must also prepare to survive, evade, resist, and escape the unpredictable twists, turns, and turmoil that come with all large-scale disasters. Recognize the threats you may face ahead of time and prepare yourself accordingly. Take self-defense classes, get firearms training, and mentally prepare yourself for the possibility that you may have to fight to defend your life or the lives of your loved ones against man and beast. When a disaster strikes, do all you can to avoid danger and violence, but outfit your BOV with tools and weapons in case trouble seeks you out.

9 ▶ STORAGE SOLUTIONS

IT'S IMPORTANT TO TAKE SOME TIME and think about how (and where) you should store and organize the supplies you're packing into a BOV. With a small BOV or large family, getting everything on board can be a logistical challenge in and of itself. In this chapter, I will discuss several BOV storage options. These will include exterior storage ideas as well as solutions for packing and organizing gear inside your vehicle.

Packing a BOV is very unique in that making it to your destination is never a guarantee. You may have to abandon your vehicle and travel on foot. This fact must be considered during your entire BOV build. Abandoning your vehicle means one (or a combination) of the following scenarios are likely to happen:

- You can take some items with you.
- You can hide items in a storage cache away from your vehicle.
- You can lock up items in a more secure storage solution inside your BOV.
- You can leave items unsecured in your BOV.

Before I begin, this is a good time for me to describe my Four-Phase System for bugging out in a BOV. How I store and organize my gear is an important factor in this system and you may want to consider something similar if it makes sense for your situation. The concept behind this system is planning for potential setbacks.

Phase One: The Bug Out Vehicle. This phase is simple. I start any Bug Out in my BOV. All of my gear is packed inside. Ideally, I make it to my Bug Out Location in my BOV without issue and never have to worry about Phases Two, Three, or Four.

Phase Two: The Bug Out Bike. If for some reason I cannot continue a Bug Out Journey in my BOV, I resort to Phase Two. This phase consists of my Yuba Mundo Cargo pedal bike loaded with supplies. I will also bring my compact folding two-wheeled Bug Out Deer Cart (discussed later in chapter fourteen), which I can pull as a small trailer on my bike. I hate the idea of abandoning everything in my BOV except for my BOB. I know several individuals who include smaller vehicles, such as ATVs or motorcycles, in their BOV for exactly this purpose. I don't have the space for another vehicle, but I do have the space for a bicycle and my Bug Out Cart. These two items combined can still carry an insane amount of gear and supplies if necessary.

Phase Three: The Bug Out Cart. If for some reason I cannot continue a Bug Out Journey on my Bug Out Bike with trailer, I resort to Phase Three.

This phase includes continuing on foot with my Bug Out Bag and my Bug Out Deer Cart. I can comfortably pull up to 150 pounds (68 kg) of gear on this cart over rugged terrain. I'll never have to pull that much weight, but it's nice to know that I can. It's designed to pull dead deer out of the woods. Others, especially those with children, may consider a stroller or wagon for this phase. Neither is ideal for rugged terrain but both are better suited for toting small children. If for some reason the distance, terrain, or other circumstances prevent me from being able to travel with a Bug Out Cart, then I resort to Phase Four.

Phase Four: Bug Out Bag and Hidden Caches. In this phase, I will abandon everything except for my Bug Out Bag and whatever I can carry with my hands. However, as I describe in the next section, I include storage containers in my BOV that I can use as hidden caches if necessary. I plan on hiding my extra supplies if I have to ditch my BOV, Bug Out Bike, and Bug Out Cart, and continue only on foot with my Bug Out Bag. An abandoned and exposed BOV, Bike, or Cart will certainly be at risk for looting and vandalizing. Hiding a secret cache of survival supplies gives you the option of retrieving them later if desired.

Creek's Yuba Mundo Cargo Bike outfitted for a Bug Out

Creek pulling Bug Out Deer Cart through overgrown field

Some terrain is Bug-Out-Bag only (Creek is holding a folding bow from goprimalnow.com)

The following is a discussion of a variety of BOV storage solutions with this four-phase philosophy in mind.

INTERIOR STORAGE SOLUTIONS

There are countless ways to store BOV supplies. Regardless of what system you choose, BOV storage items should be:

- well organized, labeled and easy to find
- hidden out of site to prevent easy theft and wandering eyes from good guys and bad guys
- packed in durable cacheable containers (at least the items you plan on taking with you or hiding if your BOV breaks down or can't continue for some other reason)

Plastic Buckets

Thick plastic buckets are great catch-all storage containers. They are cheap, durable, and fairly easy to transport. When fitted with a gamma seal lid, five-gallon buckets are airtight and waterproof. These can be purchased from practically any hardware store.

Portability: Plastic five-gallon buckets are bulky but extremely durable. They can be difficult to strap onto a bike or cart because of the round odd shape. A quick tip is to use adhesive sandpaper or grip tape designed for slippery stairs to provide traction for the bungee cords or ratcheting straps. The handles make them fairly easy to carry but extra padding is suggested.

Pros:

- cheap
- durable
- five-gallon buckets with gamma seal lids are waterproof
- nondescript

SURVIVAL CACHE

A survival cache is a secret hidden stash of survival supplies. Caches can be buried, hidden in plain sight, or stuffed into a hollow tree. The popular activity of geocaching is based on the concept of hiding secret caches. There are no rules for hiding survival caches other than cached containers should be watertight and camouflaged.

Five-gallon bucket cache hidden in hollow tree

Three of Creek's bucket containers

Thick plastic black toolbox style tote with pad lock option

Cons:
- bulky
- take up a lot of space
- not secure

Plastic Totes and Coolers

Not all totes are created equal. Avoid the thin brittle plastic versions available at most office stores. The corners bust out of these very easily. Also avoid those with the folding, interlocking lids. These aren't water-resistant and don't hold up well under weight. Save these for storing old Christmas decorations under your bed.

Look for thick durable totes with sturdy lids. I bought one tote designed for keeping tools in the back of a pickup truck that even has a place for a padlock when the lid is closed. I bolted this one to the floor of my pickup and use it as a "safe box" for more valuable items, such as tools and my propane stove. Even though

GAMMA SEAL LID

Change out the lids on your five-gallon buckets to reusable and resealable gamma seal lids. Gamma seal lids convert your five-gallon buckets to airtight and watertight containers that are great for outdoor caches. These can be spray-painted to blend in with surroundings or even buried with the top rim an inch or so out of the ground for quick and easy access later.

Gamma seal lid

Old, but solid, cooler repurposed for Bug Out storage

Vittles Vault storage containers

it's plastic, a significant amount of effort would be required to gain entry.

I've also found old coolers to be incredible Bug Out storage containers. They're lightweight, very water-resistant (not watertight), durable, insulated (from hot and cold), have a drain hole if necessary, and typically have a fairly secure clasp. I've found old coolers at garage sales for less than five dollars and they are far superior to any plastic tote that I've bought from an office supply or general merchandise store. They also don't look like a typical storage container, which can be a positive feature. But, they do look like coolers, which can be bad if others are looking for food and water. I camo spray-paint my storage coolers (shown later).

There is also a product called the Vittles Vault that is designed to store bulk pet food. It is air- and watertight. These make great BOV storage totes. They're crush-resistant, durable, food-grade, stackable, earth tone in color, and come in a variety of sizes. These would make excellent weatherproof cache containers for just about anything.

Portability: Square or rectangular totes are easier to strap onto backup BOVs such as carts and bikes than round five-gallon buckets. However, they are much more cumbersome to carry on foot, especially if they are heavy at all. These should not be considered as a "travel by foot" container.

Pros:
- durable
- hold a lot of gear
- easy to find
- stuff into tight spaces and store well

Cons:
- most do not have waterproof seals
- some can be expensive
- bulky and tricky to transport without BOV
- not secure

Military Surplus Cases

The military is always in Bug Out mode, and most of their products are designed to withstand the worst conditions. Shopping at an Army/Navy surplus store every now and then is never a bad idea. You will occasionally find surplus storage boxes and containers designed to ship and/or store electronics, ammunition, and weapons. I've picked up a couple really nice Pelican brand cases this way. Metal surplus ammo cans make excellent storage containers and organizers for ammunition and other smaller tools and parts. You can, of course, find these types of products online as well,

but shipping is never cheap for large bulky storage totes. I have also found several surplus containers (including fuel jerry cans) locally on Craigslist. I keep a variety of Bug Out ammunition in a surplus metal military ammo can behind the seat of my BOV.

Portability: While military surplus containers can be heavy because of their extremely durable qualities, they are designed with shipping and transport in mind. Consequently, I've found that surplus cases stack and pack very well. They also often have additional tie-down anchors or handles that make securing them to a cart or bike very practical. They are

SURVIVAL QUICK TIP

Pack your gear in multi-environment containers. You may have to abandon your BOV, and it's important that any gear you wish to take with you is protected from inclement weather and harsh travel environments. Durable waterproof containers that can fend off a variety of disaster-related weather conditions give you added security when transporting expensive or sensitive survival gear.

Do not use cardboard boxes or the cheap two-flap plastic office filing totes to store Bug Out Supplies. These will not hold up to the conditions that any Bug Out disaster will present.

Creek pulling Bug Out Cart through muddy stream

Surplus metal ammo can with 12-gauge, .22, 9mm, .357 and .223 ammunition

SealLine Dry Bags from www.seallinegear.com

almost always watertight and nearly crush resistant.

Pros:

- durable
- keep gear/supplies dry and protected
- designed for rugged Bug Out conditions
- some designed to accept pad locks

Cons:

- be sure to inspect all seals and corners for crack or leaks before purchase
- hard to find locally
- online shipping can be pricey

Dry Bags

In the event you have to abandon your BOV, it's important to think about protecting water-sensitive tools, clothes, and gear in case it rains or you have to make river or water crossings. This is especially true if you don't have some solid storage totes. Dry bags are primarily used in the water sports industry and are designed to keep gear dry. The only downfall is that they will also keep water *in*. Wet gear stuffed into dry bags *will not* dry out.

Thick trash compactor bags or contractor-grade trash bags make suitable (but not nearly as durable) dry bags. Twist the top a few times, fold over in a *U* shape, and tie off to keep water out. I've used these before to line my backpack when camping and also as a waterproof lining in my Bug Out Bag.

Portability: Comparatively, dry-bags are probably the least durable Bug Out Container I'm suggesting and are much more susceptible to puncture, tears, or burn holes. However, they can be very easy to strap onto a cart or bike. Strapping across a bag of items is much easier than across a rigid tote or

Small interior multifunctional gun safe

Exterior storage shelf mounted to vehicle's 2-inch (5cm) receiver

bucket and they stay very secure even over bumpy terrain.

Pros:

- durable (as compared to many other options)
- keep gear/supplies dry
- stuff into tight spaces and store well

Cons:

- will keep wet gear wet—no airflow
- susceptible to puncture
- not secure

Secure Storage

Locked and hardened storage boxes or cases can provide an added layer of security should you have to abandon your vehicle and leave some supplies behind. Even if your vehicle is abandoned, looters may not have the tools or time to access locked storage boxes. A variety of truck toolboxes are manufactured to store tools and

supplies in the back of pickup trucks like the one I mentioned earlier that I use. These also come in metal versions that can be nearly impossible to compromise. Even though they are designed for pickup trucks, I've seen several people mount these inside an SUV for secure interior storage.

Smaller "car safes" can be mounted inside the back of SUVs or even the trunks of small cars. I have a small one mounted to the center floor console where I lock up extra radios and valuables when I leave the truck. These vary in size and price and are available at many hunting supply stores. Many of them are designed to store firearms. Splitting supplies among several smaller locked storage boxes requires more time and effort for looters to steal your supplies than one large container. It's important to mount these boxes using anchors that actually screw into the metal floor,

The B*O*S*S* (Bug Out Survival Shelter) from www.gearupcenter.com comes fully stocked with Bug Out Gear

Two-inch (5cm) receiver mounted bike rack

panels, and/or frame of your vehicle. A locked box provides no security if it isn't securely attached to the vehicle from inside the box itself.

EXTERIOR STORAGE SOLUTIONS

Fitting everything inside your BOV may not be possible. Luckily, there are many different exterior storage solutions for vehicles of all types and sizes.

Tow Package/Hitch

The addition of a standard tow package with 2-inch (5cm) receiver opens up several exterior storage options. Many preppers choose to pull a trailer packed with Bug Out supplies. Some companies even specialize in trailers designed specifically for harsh off-road environments. Bug Out Trailers are discussed in more detail later. A tow package gives you the option of pulling a trailer, boat, or camper if that's something you wish to consider.

There are also a huge variety of cargo carriers that mount using a standard tow hitch. From bike racks and motorized wheelchair dollies to enclosed trunks and wire mesh baskets, there is a tow hitch storage solution to fit almost any need. These can be a great storage solution for items that don't need to be within immediate reach during a Bug Out, such as wood, tow chains, extra fuel cans, and hand tools.

Roof Racks and Rooftop Cargo Carriers

Roof racks are perfect for storing overflow Bug Out supplies that don't require quick access. A locking rooftop carrier can protect your gear from theft, inclement weather, and accidental loss (such as falling off your vehicle as you are driving). Rooftop carriers come in a variety of sizes and shapes to fit almost any storage need.

In addition to enclosed cargo carriers, roof racks are perfect for mounting tons of other Bug Out related gear, such as bicycles, canoes, kayaks, carts, wagons, shovels, axes, strollers, and off-road lights. Roof racks make it possible to bring large and bulky items that would not otherwise be possible. I've got a Bug Out Pack Canoe (discussed in more detail later) from www.oldtowncanoe.com strapped to the roof rack of my truck cap.

Don't forget high-quality bungee cords and ratcheting straps to keep your gear secure. I use only LoopRope bungee cords (www.looprope.com). They are a heavy-duty bungee cord with multiple anchor points and carabiner clips that result in a multifunctional tie-down strapping solution. I've used LoopRopes on bikes, trucks, ATVs, canoes, and even around the campsite for clotheslines and shelter guy lines. When it comes to strapping down big bulky equipment, be sure to use ratcheting straps. These ratchet down tight and hold heavy awkward loads in place.

Truck Caps

Pickup trucks, like mine, are very limited on interior storage space. For single-bench seat trucks that do not

SkyBox Cargo Box from www.yakima.com

Bug Out Pack Canoe from www.oldtowncanoe.com

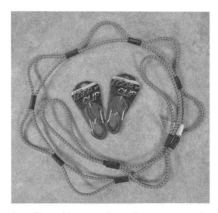

LoopRope bungees (www.looprope.com)

have an extended cab or quad cab, a truck cap is great way to extend storage into the truck bed. I did this with a locking aluminum cap that I bought used on Craigslist for a couple hundred bucks. I spray-painted it with black grill paint to match the other black features of my truck. It has locking side access panels as well as locking back doors with windows that are backed with heavy-gauge wire mesh to prevent break-ins. I added extra reinforced padlocks on each door to further deter break-ins. Most of my personal Bug Out storage is under the truck cap including my Bug Out Bike, Bug Out Deer Cart, maintenance tools, extra water, food, and three spare tires.

Ratcheting tie-down straps for securing bulky loads

Used truck caps can be found locally for very cheap and provide a protected area for bulk storage and even sleeping, if necessary. I have friends who plan on bugging out with a variety of animals including chickens and goats. A truck cap is an ideal solution for this particular scenario. It keeps the animals contained, protected, and out of the interior cargo space. I call this Noah's Truck.

A view into Creek's BOV truck cap

FUEL STORAGE

In large-scale disasters where mass exodus occurs, gas stations become watering holes of complete desperation and chaos. Even during the

Standard truck cap on F-150

DIY SPRAY-PAINT CAMOUFLAGE

Looking for an easy and effective way to spray-paint an effective camouflage pattern on your caches, vehicle, or gear? Use Mother Nature! Start by spraying on an earth tone base like dark green, tan, or brown. Next, trace real tree leaves on paper and cut them out with a razor knife. Make several templates using leaves from different trees. Then, using other earth tone colors and your templates, spray a mixed pattern of leaves on the object. This makes a very believable break-up pattern that doesn't break the bank. Be sure to use a good quality matte camo paint. I used the camo spray paint from Hunter's Specialties at www.hunterspec.com to paint this garage sale cooler I bought for two dollars, which now stores survival supplies.

Cooler before paint

Cooler with base coat of earth tone color

Multiple leaf templates

Finished camo painted cooler ready to stash

September 11th terrorist attacks, gas stations here in rural Indiana were jammed with people panicked about fuel shortages. I can remember driving by a gas station listening to the honking horns and people screaming out their windows. It was crazy. Do yourself a favor and make preparations to avoid these potential hotspots of human interaction and confrontation.

Ideally, you should have enough fuel in your tank and in on-board fuel cans to get you to your BOL without stopping for gas. I actually recommend having at least twice what is needed to make the trip just in case you get stuck in traffic or have to make costly detours. Both are very likely.

Never let the fuel gauge on your BOV fall under three-quarters of a tank when going about your daily routine. Having a nearly full tank of gas at all times assures you have at least that much gas when starting a Bug Out. It takes ten gallons of fuel for me to get to my BOL. I keep thirty gallons of fuel in my BOV at all times—three times what I need. This includes a twenty-gallon gas tank and two five-gallon jerry cans. You may require on-board fuel storage as well. I've chosen to use metal jerry cans but plastic fuel cans are available as well. I have these mounted to the side of my truck with locking hardware

to prevent theft. I also found a used jerry can locally on Craigslist.com for twenty dollars that I keep secured inside the truck cap with a strap. I prefer to keep all of my fuel storage outside the vehicle interior and recommend you do the same for obvious reasons. No matter how nice your gas cans are, fuel stinks and can give you a serious headache if kept inside. Not to mention that it's dangerous to keep fuel inside the vehicle as well. Roof racks are a great place to store a couple fuel cans. You can run inexpensive bicycle cable locks through the fuel can handle and around the roof rack frame to prevent theft. It's not foolproof but will prevent someone from pulling off a quick grab-and-dash fuel heist.

Whenever you store fuel long term, you need to use a fuel stabilizer. The product I use is STA-BIL from www.sta-bil.com. STA-BIL extends the life of fuel to a full year. This prevents you having to worry about whether your fuel is good or bad. Just use your fuel storage once a year and you'll be good to go at all times. One advantage of diesel fuel is that it stores for much longer than gasoline. By adding a biocide to prevent algae growth, diesel fuel will store for many years. Combine that with a product like STA-BIL and you can expect to get a shelf life of ten-plus years out of diesel.

Five-gallon fuel jerry can mounted and secured with padlock to exterior of Creek's BOV

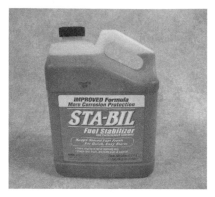

STA-BIL fuel stabilizer

SUMMARY

Fuel storage should be at the top of your storage priorities. Without fuel, nothing else matters. Beyond that, the gear in your BOV should be compartmentalized, organized, and easy to find. Durable multi-environment containers allow you to cache or transport extra supplies should you have to abandon your vehicle en route to your BOL. Don't cut corners on storage containers. No one wants to spend their hard-earned money on a container, but rugged containers capable of withstanding demanding environments are important and can last a lifetime.

SURVIVAL QUICK TIP

Don't' forget fuel for your gasoline-powered tools, such as generators and chainsaws. I keep one gallon of unleaded gasoline for my generator and one gallon of gas/oil mix for the chainsaw securely strapped in the back of my truck at all times.

One-gallon gas can for gasoline-powered generator

10 ▸ DEMYSTIFYING THE ELECTROMAGNETIC PULSE

IF YOU'VE BEEN RESEARCHING survival and preparedness for very long at all, you've at least heard the acronym "EMP." EMP stands for electromagnetic pulse. It's been the theme behind many popular survival books and television series in recent months. In order to understand how this phenomenon can affect your preparedness efforts (particularly your BOV), you must first understand what it is, what causes it, and its potential effects to life as we know it.

WHAT IS AN EMP?

Simply put, an EMP is a very high pulse of electromagnetic radiation, typically high above the Earth's surface. EMPs can be man-made or natural. The massive disruption in the electrical and magnetic fields caused by an EMP can produce overwhelming surges in electrical voltage and current.

WHAT CAUSES AN EMP?

I will discuss our two largest threats: nuclear EMP attacks and solar storms. Both emit a surge of electromagnetic waves we refer to as an EMP. Nuclear EMPs are caused by detonating a nuclear bomb miles above the Earth's surface. This kind of EMP is the most powerful and can have crippling effects (discussed in detail next) for hundreds and even thousands of miles. Solar events, including solar storms, geomagnetic storms, solar flares, and coronal mass ejections, can also cause a damaging EMP. Mankind has limited experience with both types of EMP, even with intentional research. There are

Two awesome BOVs

only a handful of occurrences (both combined) from which to draw reliable data.

OUR DEPENDENCY ON ELECTRICITY AND ELECTRONICS

The United States is unquestionably dependent on electricity. We have eagerly welcomed all of the conveniences it provides. All of our infrastructure systems depend on a reliable electric power grid and all of the little circuits and components that magically weave it all together. Our entire society depends on it—*everything*! Water, food, fuel, communication, transportation, Internet, medical service, emergency service, public safety, financial transactions, information networks, and government services all depend on electricity and none of them can operate effectively without it, especially long term. It is electricity that allows our three hundred-plus million citizens to survive. And, it is electricity that has enabled our population to get that big to begin with.

GAME CHANGER

An EMP threatens life as we know it. It is one of the few complete and total game-changing events. The surge of voltage and current caused by an EMP has the potential to disrupt or damage virtually any kind of "unshielded" electronic equipment, including but not limited to the electrical power grid, telecommunication systems, computers, circuits, relays, and all electronic fuel pumps. Large EMP events can affect areas hundreds and even thousands of miles in diameter. Even a smaller regional burst can have devastating consequences as the ripples of outages slowly break down our tightly interwoven national infrastructure systems.

Recent disasters are only a taste of what to expect if an EMP strikes our country. Hurricane Katrina will look like a walk in the park. The 1977 New York blackouts and resulting uncontrollable looting and riots which *Time* magazine dubbed "The Night of Terror"? We'll beg for times that glorious.

As far as potential disasters go, a large-scale EMP is as bad as it gets. Most disasters last at most a few days. Cleanup and recovery may last several months, but history reports that the disaster itself is typically over within 72 hours. An EMP is different. The pulse itself is just the beginning. Best estimates from professionals and experts who have reported to Congress after years of studying our nation's vulnerabilities to EMP say that the affected areas can be expected to be without power-dependent services (virtually everything) for many months and potentially years.

In fact, a committee of expert scientists was commissioned by congress right after the September 11th terror attacks to investigate the threat of EMP in America. In this report to the Committee of Armed Services for the House of Representatives in July 2004 (find the transcript at http://commdocs.house.gov/committees/security/has204000.000/has204000_0.htm#26), it was suggested that a large-scale EMP could feasibly shrink the current population to one-third of its size and that the fatalities would be much more numerous than from a ground-level attack with a nuclear bomb. Participants in that hearing likened an EMP to a time machine that would thrust America back a full century in technology. This excerpt from that report says it best:

"*The population that this continent carried late in the nineteenth century, sir, was almost a factor of ten smaller than it is at the present time. We went from where we had 70 percent of the population on the farms feeding 30 percent of the people in the villages and cities to where 3 percent of the population on the farms at the present time feeds the other 97 percent of the country.*"

So just looking at it from an agricultural and food supply standpoint, if we were no longer able to fuel our agricultural machine in this country, the food production of the country would simply stop because we do not have the horses and mules that used to tow the agricultural gear around in the 1880s and 1890s.

The devastation that would accompany this massive shrink in populous through starvation, dehydration, violence, and lack of medical services is unspeakable and impossible to put into words, even for the most imaginative fiction author. Nothing you've ever read or seen in the movies can even compare.

PROBABILITY OF OCCURRENCE

Geomagnetic solar storm EMPs have already occurred. One of the most notable was in 1989 that knocked down the Hydro-Québec power grid and left six million people without power for almost two weeks. Mother Nature is a brutal adversary and her weapons are vast. I wish, though, that she was our only concern.

Several countries have the nukes and delivery systems to make an EMP attempt over U.S. soil. Ever heard the term "Scud missile"? Sure you have, it's a common phrase thrown around when discussing modern warfare. It's not only a common phrase but a common weapon. Almost any rogue faction and certainly a ticked-off country can get their hands on one without too much effort (or already have them). It's no secret that these Scud missiles can deliver a high-altitude nuclear bomb over America from almost anywhere in the vast ocean that surrounds us. This makes the launch location difficult to track and locate. An EMP is the ultimate terrorist attack, and the devastating effect of one on electronic infrastructure is common knowledge. We live in a crazy world with a lot of crazy people, many of whom have a grudge against America. Rogue states like North Korea and Iran are obvious threats. Nuclear states such as Russia and China must be acknowledged as well. The threat of an EMP attack or geomagnetic solar storm is growing every day.

In my opinion, an EMP attack is the greatest threat to life as we know it in modern America. However, with all of that said, the probability of an EMP occurring is still very low. Even if an EMP of some kind does happen, there are still many questions as to how the effects will play out. Furthermore, the damage from an EMP depends on many factors including altitude of event, strength of blast, location of electronics, and shielding. In the realm of disaster preparedness, they are many other more likely events to worry about. Few, though, have the damaging potential of an EMP.

HOW WORRIED SHOULD I BE ABOUT AN EMP?

That's a good question. I try to consider all potential disasters in my preparedness efforts but I definitely spend more time, money, and energy preparing for the ones that are more likely to happen. An EMP is not high on that list for me but I still do include it as a possibility. (Remember, I own a survival and disaster preparedness training facility after all. I probably think more about this stuff than most.) This is why I've chosen the early 1980s model truck as my BOV and really the only reason I've chosen that old truck at all—besides, maybe, the fact that it is affordable. Modern vehicles are unquestionably more reliable. I've made this BOV EMP-proof by eliminating all electronic components. Furthermore, I do keep a variety of electronic devices in an EMP-shielding Faraday cage (discussed later in this chapter). Preparing for an EMP is a fairly extreme measure and, in all honesty, there is a lot to be done before one should consider EMP preps.

One thing I've learned over the years is that different people prepare for different reasons. Who am I to question what events others prepare for and why? An EMP is a number one priority for some and not even on the radar for others. Nonetheless, it is a popular topic of conversation among survival-minded individuals and even more popular when discussing BOVs. At the very minimum, it's good to at least be somewhat educated on the topic. Even I still have much to learn. EMP is certainly not my forte of expertise.

HOW DOES AN EMP AFFECT MY BOV?

Any electronic component in your BOV is susceptible to EMP damage. That's scary—especially for those who drive modern vehicles (late 1990s and up). Why? Modern vehicles are filled with electronic components that control everything from ignition to fuel injection to brakes.

The computerized electronic component movement began in the early 1980s. Most vehicles produced before then did not include electronic components. Early vehicles had a points ignition, manual fuel pump, and carburetor. Now, cars are essentially a computer with wheels. If the computer goes down, the car doesn't run—period. Hybrid electric cars are especially screwed. In general, there are three basic categories.

General Category 1: Pre-1980s

Most pre-1980s vehicles without electronic components are considered EMP safe. If you own a pre-1980s

vehicle and are concerned about EMP vulnerabilities, ask your mechanic if there are any electronic components on your vehicle. If there are, consider ordering replacement components and storing them in a shielded Faraday cage just in case (instructions at the end of this chapter). Or, better yet, configure a nonelectronic/mechanical workaround altogether and bypass those parts.

General Category 2: Early Electronic Component Vehicles

The computerized components in the early phases of integration were very basic. They typically controlled single systems, such as ignition. These components can be ordered and replaced by most anyone who is comfortable under the hood of a car. Some, though, require special programming. If your vehicle fits this description, consider ordering replacement components and storing them in a shielded Faraday cage just in case (instructions at the end of this chapter). Have a conversation with a trusted mechanic first about how realistic it would be for you to just "swap out" fried components.

General Category 3: Modern Computerized Vehicles

If you own a modern computerized vehicle (which most of the general

Engine in Creek's 1985 diesel pickup

**Engine in Creek's brother's 2012 Jeep
(Don't worry, Mike, I'll come pick you up!)**

population does) and an EMP strikes, I hope you're in good physical shape because there is certainly a chance your car isn't moving unless you live on a really steep hill. The line between electronic components and mechanical components in modern vehicles is blurred. It's hard, especially for the average untrained person, to define where one ends and the other begins. Everything is controlled by electronic components, including ignition, brakes, fuel injection, dash controls, windows, emissions, lights, and the list goes on and on. It is nearly impossible to swap out backup electronic parts in these highly complex vehicles. If EMP is at the top of the list of why you are prepping, my advice is don't buy a modern vehicle.

EMP PROTECTION: FARADAY CAGE

Whether you want to protect backup electronics for your vehicle or other tools, such as radios, cell phones, and battery chargers, you'll need to shield them from the pulse of electromagnetic radiation. Fortunately, there is a pretty simple and cheap way to do this.

The Faraday Cage

Named after scientist Michael Faraday, the Faraday cage is simply a shield of conductive material (metal) that surrounds the items you want to protect. This shield blocks and diverts the pulse from reaching your electronics. I've seen all kinds of homemade Faraday cages over the years. Some are cardboard boxes wrapped in aluminum foil. Others are wooden boxes surrounded in metal mesh. The simplest and easiest in my opinion is an insulated galvanized metal bucket with tight-fitting lid. There can't be any gaps or openings. The lid must fit tightly and securely, and I even wrap the seal with some aluminum tape that you can buy at any hardware store. I use the following three steps when assembling my Faraday Cage.

Step 1: Insulate the metal container. Your electronics need to be insulated from the metal container. A simple way to do this is to line the container with cardboard. I insert a tube of cardboard and then pad the bottom with packing paper. Make sure there is no metal can showing.

Step 2: Double wrap. Next, I wrap each of my electronic devices in aluminum foil and then again in thick butcher paper as an added layer of security. This is in essence a mini Faraday cage within the larger cage. A second layer never hurts and it doesn't take up much extra time or money.

Step 3: Seal it up. After packing my electronic components inside, I fill the empty space with butcher paper to pack everything nice and tight. This also provides a layer of insulation from the lid. Then I seal all the way around the lid with a couple layers of aluminum tape. Below is a non-exhaustive list of items one may want to consider for EMP shielding:

- two-way radios
- shortwave radio
- handheld CB radio
- solar battery chargers and batteries
- LED flashlights

Small galvanized metal bucket lined with cardboard and packing paper

Electronics being wrapped in foil and then paper

Tight-fitting lid sealed with aluminum tape

A few EMP-vulnerable components

- cordless drill/charger
- tablcts/e-readers
- electronic medical equipment
- spare fuses

SUMMARY

Even I am not overly invested in the idea of an EMP attack or occurrence. Many of my general "off-grid" preps, such as a hand-pump water well, wood-burning stove, and backyard garden serve as indirect EMP preps, although EMP has never been my motivating factor for preparedness. I believe you should prepare for the disasters that are most likely to happen in your area. These include natural and man-made. If you live near a nuclear power plant, you should prepare for a potential meltdown and sudden evacuation. If you live in New York or Washington, D.C., you should prepare for terrorist attacks and the mess that comes with those. If you live in tornado alley, you should prepare for tornadoes. If you live in hurricane country, you should prepare for the next Katrina. Prepare for what's most probable first and then expand into less likely events as time, money, and other resources allow. History can absolutely help predict the future.

11 ▶ BUG OUT VEHICLES

THE NEXT FIVE CHAPTERS are dedicated to highlighting, reviewing, and evaluating a huge variety of BOV options. These will include everything from traditional vehicles, planes, boats, wheeled carts, and many options in between. While it's impossible to include absolutely every vehicle option, I've been able to amass an impressive list, that will cover most any circumstance, environment, or lifestyle. I've done my best to outline the pros, cons, and special considerations for each type of vehicle. This chapter will deal primarily with traditional motorized passenger vehicles, starting with cars.

PASSENGER CARS

There are more cars on the road than any other type of vehicle. However, "cars" is a vast category and not all cars are created equal. Some cars, like the all-wheel drive Subaru, take pride in their "off the beaten path" capability. Others, like the Toyota Prius, will travel significantly farther than my gas-guzzling diesel truck on significantly less fuel. Still yet, when you need to get out of Dodge at a high rate of speed, Mustangs and Camaros will be at the head of the pack. Station wagons excel in storage room while Smart Cars and MINI Coopers can thread traffic needles. My dad's Buick will blend into the masses, but my buddy's Dodge Viper is a Bug Out Bull's-eye on wheels. There are so many choices and all of them have pros and cons. In general, below are the pros and cons for the "car" category.

Pros

Fuel: With a few fast-moving exceptions, cars excel in the miles traveled versus fuel consumed category. This is an obvious advantage.

Jake's Bug Out Subaru Outback

A car that blends into the crowd is a good thing

This car has just a few inches of ground clearance.

Smart Car perfect for tight traffic squeezes

Blending: My truck (and many of the BOVs featured in pictures throughout this book) will stand out in a sea of vehicles. This is a disadvantage. An average car will blend and be less of a target.

Replacement Parts: With some exceptions, replacement parts are reasonably accessible for many popular makes and models in this category.

Cons

Off-Road: Cars do not do well off-road.

Clearance: Most cars have little road clearance. In a Bug Out environment, more clearance is almost always better.

Storage: Most cars have very limited storage apace. One must plan ahead to organize and pack Bug Out Gear.

Special Considerations

- All-wheel drive is better than two-wheel drive.

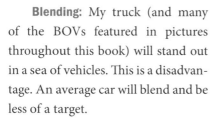

- Front-wheel drive is more effective than rear-wheel drive in snow and most off-road conditions.

PICKUP TRUCKS

I love pickup trucks. In recent years, pickups have become much more feature-rich and comfortable than they used to be. Extended cabs and quad cabs provide a surprising amount of interior space for hauling people and gear. Caps, bed covers, and campers can be added to provide an incredible amount of secure storage for all kinds of Bug Out tools, gear, supplies, and even smaller vehicles (like a Bug Out Bike or four-wheeler). Four-wheel drive trucks are excellent off-road machines. Two-wheel drive pickup trucks are cheaper, but are among the worst off-road vehicles on planet Earth. Two-wheel drive pickups

ICON FJ45 from www.icon4x4.com

are rear-wheel drive. The back end of a pickup truck is really light and with no weight on the rear wheels, they get stuck really easily. I used to have a two-wheel drive pickup and it would literally get stuck in wet grass. It was unbelievable. I will never own one again.

Other modern developments include hybrid trucks with fuel efficiency that will rival some medium-sized cars. Even my old diesel gets mileage per gallon in the high teens. Unlike my older pickup, modern trucks are incredibly comfortable to drive. My truck feels like a soapbox car with wooden wheels and is a completely different experience from trucks with modern suspensions and features designed to make bumpy rides more comfortable.

Regardless of the nearly limitless number of features available, trucks of all shapes, sizes, makes, and models make excellent BOVs options.

Pros

Storage: Trucks have a larger storage capacity than most modern vehicles. They are specifically designed to haul lots of stuff.

Hard Use: Most trucks are designed for work and excel in "off the pavement" environments (if they are four-wheel drive). They typically have higher ground clearance and beefy suspensions.

Power: While many cars boast fuel economy, trucks are best known for power. Most trucks have engines to match the brutal demands of their hardworking owners. Trucks can pull heavy loads and power through harsh off-road conditions. Whether it's yanking a fallen tree off the road or

Truck with camper from www.fourwh.com

fording a flooded road, many trucks will be up for the task.

Off-Road: Most trucks have a 4x4 option (don't buy one that doesn't) and will perform well off the pavement if necessary.

Cons

Access: Be sure to keep your quick access gear in the cab if possible. Access to storage in the truck bed requires you to exit the vehicle. This may not always be ideal.

Exposure: Unless protected by a bed cover, camper, or cap, all exterior storage items must be in waterproof containers to shed rain and other elements.

Fuel: Fuel efficiency is almost always lower than smaller cars.

Security: Any items kept in the bed are more susceptible to theft. Consider secure storage options.

SPORT UTILITY VEHICLES (SUVS) AND JEEPS

I believe SUVs and Jeeps represent the most practical and realistic class of BOVs available on the market today. Jeeps are in a class all their own, and I don't necessarily consider them an SUV, but for brevity have included them in this category nonetheless. Many will argue that the Jeep (Wrangler) is the best off-road vehicle available and I wouldn't necessarily disagree, especially when comparing mid-priced vehicles.

The majority of off-road accessory websites and catalogs cater specifically to Jeep enthusiasts. This speaks to the popularity of that vehicle for adventure travel. An insane amount of off-road aftermarket accessories are available for Jeeps. Nearly all of these accessories are applicable to a Bug Out Scenario.

Jeep Wrangler

SUV on rugged terrain

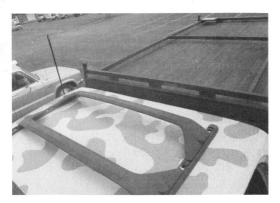

My repurposed, cut-down salvaged roof rack

Much larger roof cage on H1 Hummer

SUVs in general do a great job of capturing the best of both the car and truck worlds. While they don't get the gas mileage of a smaller car, they do have more interior storage space and better ground clearance and off-road abilities (oftentimes four-wheel drive). Many SUVs are equally as capable off the pavement as any comparable pickup truck. In fact, I can't think of a reason to purchase a truck over an SUV other than if you absolutely needed the large truck bed for hauling something that just can't fit inside an SUV.

I traveled the entire country one summer just out of college and lived out of my compact two-door Ford Explorer Sport SUV. I sheltered in that old truck for weeks at a time in almost every condition imaginable: on the beach, in parking lots, at rest stops, in the woods, on mountainsides, in hot weather, in cold weather,

and in inclement weather. Once I figured out a system, it wasn't all that bad. It was even fairly comfortable to sleep in (diagonally), which I can't say for any of the trucks or cars I've ever owned. Those have all been awful. I wish I had a picture of that Explorer to show you in this book. It was my BOV at the time.

One advantage of an SUV over trucks and cars is the size of the roof. A large roof allows for a large roof rack. I couldn't even find a roof rack for my current truck and had to salvage one from a wrecked Explorer at the junkyard and cut it down to fit. Even then it had to be very small to fit on the compact roof above the single bench seat. SUVs allow for ample roof storage as compared to their purebred counterparts. Safari-style roof racks have come way down in price over the years and are must have for any BOV-SUV.

Sportsmobile 4×4 Custom Camper Van from www.sportsmobile.com

Another Sportsmobile 4×4 Custom Camper Van from www.sportsmobile.com

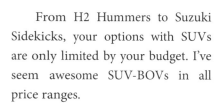

From H2 Hummers to Suzuki Sidekicks, your options with SUVs are only limited by your budget. I've seem awesome SUV-BOVs in all price ranges.

Pros

Storage: Lots of weatherproof and secure interior storage plus large roof for securing items overhead.

People: Great for families.

Off-Road: Most SUVs have a 4×4 option (don't buy one that doesn't).

Blending: My truck (and many of the BOVs featured in pictures throughout this book) will stand out in a sea of vehicles. This is a disadvantage. SUVs are very common and will be less of a target.

Cons

Top Heavy: More likely to roll over than lower profile cars and even trucks.

Fuel: Fuel efficiency is almost always lower than smaller cars.

CARGO VANS AND MINIVANS

I've owned a BOV in this category. It was a big Ford E-350 XLT Super-duty fifteen-passenger cargo van. The owner before me had sent it off to Quigley Motor Company, Inc. in Pennsylvania (www.quigley4x4.com) for a Quigley 4×4 conversion. It had a V10 gasoline engine and I could literally watch the fuel needle move. Miles per gallon was in the single digits and ended up being one of my motivating factors for ultimately selling the beast. Having owned a van-sized BOV, I learned a lot about what I liked and didn't like, which will influence my input into this category.

I've seen several stock all-wheel drive (AWD) vans over the years that would make excellent BOVs. Chevy

Volkswagon van

Cavernous interior space in fifteen-passenger cargo van

made the Astro Van for a while with AWD and Toyota has recently released the Sienna with AWD. There may be others. If choosing a van as a BOV, I would definitely consider an AWD model or even an aftermarket conversion by a company like Quigley. This option, in conjunction with some tready tires, can drastically improve your ability to navigate off the pavement around roadblocks or through snow and mud during inclement weather. Never buy a rear-wheel drive van. They will get stuck almost instantly in wet, muddy or snowy conditions.

Pros

Interior Space: Storage is by far the number-one reason to choose a van BOV. Whether to haul children or excess gear, a van has some clear advantages from the interior storage

perspective. It also makes a suitable shelter and makeshift RV if necessary. From folding back seats to floorboard storage, ample interior space is a huge advantage.

People: Great for families.

Blending: An AWD or 4×4 van just looks like a van. There are tons of vans on the road and these won't stick out unless you make them.

EarthRoamer XV-LT Adventure Vehicle from www.earthroamer.com

Nonthreatening: Vans are non-threatening. Especially if law enforcement starts trying to identify potential threats, a minivan will be in the clear and sail cleanly under the radar. My truck, however, not so much.

Fuel: Many minivans get excellent gas mileage.

Cons

Off-Road: Most vans (especially the rear-wheel drive models) perform very poorly off-road. If you can't afford or find an AWD model, try your best to choose a front-wheel drive version. Rear-wheel drive cargo vans are some of the worst off-road vehicles on the planet.

Fuel: Many eight-cylinder and ten-cylinder cargo vans get horrible gas mileage.

MOBILE HOMES AND RECREATIONAL VEHICLES (RVS)

There is a nearly infinite range of RVs BOVs. From multimillion dollar rigs to used truck cap campers, you are only limited by your budget and creativity. I've even seen families convert old school buses to mobile home style BOVs. The major difference between this category and all of the rest (except some boats) is that you have the option to live inside of them—at least short term. In most other vehicles, an overnight stay (and even bathroom

break) would typically require exiting the vehicle. This category contains vehicles that are by definition self-contained living units.

I have several friends who have decided to go the RV BOV route. As I mentioned earlier in the book, I view a BOV as a means to an end and not the end itself, but I certainly respect and understand why some survival-minded individuals like the idea of a mobile BOL/BOV combo unit. I have to admit, there is a certain allure to traveling in a self-sustaining mobile BOL (though all RVs are only temporarily self-sustaining). Aside from a complete extended societal collapse, RVs represent a great solution to evacuate a disaster zone and live on the road until it's safe to return. The idea of retreating in an RV has many advantages, but the idea of using that RV as a final BOL in an extended collapse has many limitations. It's important to note there has never been an extended collapse/disaster in the United States. All disasters have been localized and fairly short term. However, there still is simply no perfect plan no matter how much time you invest or how much money you spend.

Pros

Options: A mobile home or RV gives an evacuee many options. You aren't limited to a specific destination. The road or a good hiding spot is your home away from home.

Self-Contained: There is increased risk every time you exit a BOV. (I even keep portable potty bags in the cab of my truck to prevent having to exit in a hostile environment.) Many RVs have bathrooms, sleeping quarters, water storage, and kitchens inside. A self-contained BOV with the ability to move about inside helps with sanity on long trips as well.

Electricity: Many RVs have built-in generators that can provide electricity to charge/power batteries or electronics if possible. Often, these generators also power air conditioning and cooking appliances as well when the main engines are turned off.

Fuel: While RVs don't typically get great fuel mileage, they almost always have massive fuel tanks. These things are designed to hit the open road, and there's nothing more frustrating than having to stop for gas all the time. Large tanks allow for longer and farther travel. This travel range is a big plus for anyone bugging out in an RV. Whether sitting in traffic or driving far away from ground zero, large on-board fuel tanks are always a good thing.

Storage: RVs can not only house plenty of people but tons of supplies as well. With my truck, for example, I have to get out of the cab to access almost all of my Bug Out Supplies. This is a disadvantage. The large interior spaces of RVs allow one to keep most

MILITARY COMMUNICATION SHELTERS

Surplus slide-in military communication shelters can be purchased from resellers and individuals online for just a few hundred dollars. With a little bit of sweat equity, these can make very durable (and cool) truck campers. They have very secure locking doors and make an excellent storage or DIY camper solution for pickup trucks. I almost purchased one of these for my BOV but decided to rehab cost was a little much as compared to the cheaper aluminum shell.

Several surplus slide-in military communications shelters

everything within hands reach without having to leave the vehicle.

Cons

Maneuverability: Even small RVs can be difficult to maneuver, especially in congested traffic or in an off-road situation. Large RVs can be nearly impossible to navigate through crowded streets or wooded areas. Evacuating before mass exodus is imperative.

Off-Road: Besides the really expensive 4×4 adventure units and truck-mounted campers, RVs are not well suited for off-pavement travel. This can be a huge issue when navigating through medians or over embankments becomes necessary.

Blending: RVs don't blend well. In fact, they look like they contain a lot of supplies. RVs are absolutely more of a target to looters than other less conspicuous vehicles. They are also more difficult to camouflage if security becomes an issue.

Security: Not that traditional vehicles are defensive fortresses, but many RVs are built from wood,

SURVIVOR TRUCK

Check out the Survivor Truck! This custom BOV has a crazy list of cool survival features, including:

Survivor Truck from www.survivortruck.com

- armored command center; motion/vibration/burglar alarm; observation and sniper platform; 360-degree protective cage; 360-degree video monitoring; thermal imaging/Night Vision/Infrared lighting; NBC (Nuclear, Biological, Chemical environment) air handling and filtration system; onboard air compressor, winches front and rear
- sleeps fourteen; custom pop-up camper by Four Wheel Campers; fold-out tent for six; custom utility bed and storage system; custom interior
- CB/HAM/two-way radios, communications repeater; private encrypted radio network system; EMP-proof Faraday cage
- bi-fuel compatible (gasoline and propane); 6V /12V / propane, CNG and gasoline engine and generator; solar power/deployable solar generator, inverters; 200 amp 12V welder and power generator
- 120 gallons of water storage plus water purification/water desalination
- Rhino Linings custom coat on entire vehicle

Xtender off-road trailer/camper from www.vmioffroad.com

Tow-behind pop-up camper

plastic, and fiberglass. This is something to consider when evaluating vehicle security.

TRAILERS AND TOW-BEHIND CAMPERS

I know several people who have chosen to outfit and prepare a Bug Out Trailer versus a particular vehicle. Though this is not what I've chosen to do, I will admit that it does make a lot of sense.

Trailers are extremely versatile tools when it comes to containing and transporting Bug Out supplies and gear. I even know a guy who mounted a slide-in truck bed style camper onto a pontoon boat. This is not only a Bug Out Trailer but also a living quarters and a fully functional pontoon boat if necessary. It's a pretty cool and inventive Bug Out setup that creatively incorporates several types of vehicles.

Whether you use a two-hundred-dollar wire frame trailer from Craigslist or buy a fully stocked self-contained tow behind Bug Out Camper with bathroom and kitchen, you *must* have a vehicle capable of pulling it. This eliminates most small cars. You must also have a properly sized and installed tow package with wiring harness. Four-wheel drive trucks and SUVs with six-cylinder or larger engines are the best trailer towing candidates.

Tow-behind adventure campers like the Campa Cub and the Xtender are becoming extremely popular within the off-roading and adventure travel communities. This style of camper/trailer also doubles as an excellent Bug Out Trailer and is typically very feature-rich. Many preppers, however, like the nondescript look of a standard covered cargo trailer with the Bug Out amenities discreetly installed inside.

Campa Cub all-terrain trailer from www.campausa.com

Discreet 6×12 covered Bug Out Trailer

One of the most enticing benefits of a Bug Out Trailer is that a trailer doesn't age like a vehicle. It's not uncommon for a trailer to last a lifetime with minimum maintenance. A trailer isn't driven every day like a vehicle and doesn't have engine parts that fail with lack of use or age. A BOV is a huge investment that may one day have to be replaced because of high miles or a worn-out engine. Bug Out Trailers are rarely used and therefore last forever. Many people don't want to modify and outfit their everyday driver vehicle as a BOV and like the idea of just hitching up to a quick get-out-of-Dodge solution. I know one family who has had the same homemade Bug Out Trailer for fifteen years. It has seen several different tow vehicles come and go during that time frame. They only put the effort and money into their trailer once and now it just sits in the garage ready to go when they need it. Besides an occasional practice run or camping trip, they never use it. It will last forever.

Special Considerations

Below are a few things to consider when outfitting and storing a Bug Out Trailer:

Vehicle and Hitch: First, make sure your vehicle is capable of towing your fully loaded BOT. Then, make sure your hitch is rated for the weight as well.

Wiring: Make sure all of the lights work on your trailer. Not only are malfunctioning lights illegal, they are dangerous. The last thing you need is a rear-end collision because your brake lights weren't working.

Keep a Spare Tire: The tow vehicle spare will probably not fit the trailer. Keep a trailer spare tire or two inside the trailer. Make sure the vehicle lug wrench also fits the trailer wheel lugs.

Dry Rot: When tires sit for months without use they tend to develop dry rot, especially when exposed to sunlight. Check the trailer tires to make sure this isn't an issue. Pull the trailer at least a couple times a month to keep everything on the up-and-up.

Practice in Reverse: It's easy to tow a trailer. It's not so easy to go in reverse with one. Practice this until you become an expert at backing up with a trailer. You may have to maneuver and reverse in hectic traffic one day.

Wheel Chocks: Pick up a decent set of wheel chocks to prevent your trailer from rolling should you need to disconnect on uneven ground. Improvising with rocks and logs is dangerous.

Trailer Dolly: Just in case you get in a tight bind, it never hurts to have a trailer dolly. This allows you to quickly maneuver and rotate even very heavy trailers without the use of a vehicle. I used to set up a trailer at festivals, and trailer dollies were invaluable for helping to navigate the trailer back onto my hitch from in tight corners.

Pintle Hitch: Note that a military-style pintle hitch will be harder to steal if for some reason you have to abandon, hide, or leave your trailer. Consider choosing (or modifying) your trailer tongue with a pintle hitch. A ball/pintle combo hitch on your vehicle can pull both pintle-style and traditional ball trailers. Pintle hitches are also more secure for off-road bumpy travel and especially on sideways slopes.

Pros

Vehicle Independent: With a Bug Out Trailer, you aren't limited to just one BOV. Any vehicle that will tow the trailer will work!

Pintle hitch

Trailer dolly

Storage: Trailers offer huge storage potential. It's also much safer to store extra fuel in a trailer than in the trunk of a vehicle.

Custom: Many trailers are highly customizable and can be modified to suit almost any need. From hauling four-wheelers to rooftop solar panels, creativity is the limit.

Cache: If necessary, the entire trailer can be hidden for retrieval at a later date.

Shelter: Many survivalists have outfitted trailers to serve double-duty as a Bug Out Location living quarters with bunks, heating stove, solar panels, and even a bathroom.

Budget: Trailers are typically cheaper than dedicated BOVs.

Cons

Maneuverability: Trailers can be very difficult to maneuver in congested traffic or tight places. Backing up in these circumstances can be nearly impossible.

Off-Road: Trailers can very difficult to tow in rugged off-road environments.

Mileage: The addition of a trailer will reduce the gas mileage for any vehicle.

Access: Gear packed inside or strapped on a trailer can be cumbersome and inconvenient to access.

SUMMARY

I've learned there will always be a better BOV than the one you own. You can drive yourself crazy trying to find and purchase the perfect BOV. Trust me, a perfect one does not exist. Working with what you have and within your means will cover you for the vast majority of any threats.

Most people will choose a BOV of some type or variety from this chapter. Others may have unique circumstances that require a more specific vehicle. Let's now explore a variety of "atypical" BOVs.

12 ▸ BUG OUT BOATS

I COULD WRITE AN ENTIRE BOOK on this topic alone, but I'll do my best to keep my thoughts both brief and thorough.

You'll notice I have a canoe strapped to the top of my Bug Out Truck. Even though it looks cool, it isn't just for looks. That canoe is absolutely a part of my overall Bug Out Strategy. I have planned for an alternate water evacuation route just in case I ever need it. I live on the north side of Indianapolis in Central Indiana. Last time I checked, Indianapolis was the twelfth largest city in the country. Mass exodus is the term used to describe when everyone is evacuating a metropolitan area at the same time. This happens during every large-scale disaster in major cities. Inevitably, traditional evacuation routes (pavement roads) are blocked, especially at choke points, such as bridges and on/off ramps to major traffic arteries. The combina-

tion of accidents, empty gas tanks, and increased desperation creates a very hostile and dangerous situation. Oftentimes, roadways become completely and hopelessly gridlocked. Because I live in a metropolitan area I must consider this as a possibility. Ideally, if you can predict a Bug Out, you should get out early. I've never in my life seen a traffic-jammed river.

Consequently, I bought a house on a major river that runs through central Indiana. In fact, my Willow Haven Outdoor training facility is located on a tributary to this same river in north central Indiana. My Bug Out Location (BOL) is about a one-day hike from a location on the river several hours south of Indianapolis. This plan does involve ditching/caching my canoe at the final dock site. I'll consider it a disaster casualty. I'm okay with that. The point is that I can still get out of Dodge and closer to my

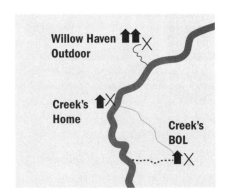

Creek's water evacuation route diagram

Creek portaging with Old Town Pack Canoe

BOL via waterway even if my BOV is trapped during mass exodus. There are several portages along the way, but my Old Town Pack Canoe is designed to be carried without too much effort.

It's amazing how you can slip through even a heavily populated city almost completely undetected by waterway, especially with a quiet canoe or kayak. There is no question that waterways are safer than roadways when it comes to threats from people. I could even travel all the way to the Gulf of Mexico from my home if I really needed. The entire eastern half of the United States is interwoven with thousands of miles of waterways that can be used for a potential Bug Out if you have a boat. Bugging Out onto large bodies of water, such as the Great Lakes or an ocean, gives an entirely new perspective to a BOV and BOL. I have a friend whose BOL is an island off the Eastern Coast of the United States. His BOV is a sailboat. This is certainly not my ideal scenario, but it's pretty cool nonetheless.

In addition to escaping a life-threatening disaster, getting far away from people is a top priority for many who are considering a Bug Out Boat. In the event of a large-scale plague or pandemic, many argue that being isolated in open water is better than being trapped on land with a contagious infection. All boats must return to

Flooded roads

land at some point, but it is certainly true that exposure to people will be less on open water. Many isolated gunkholes, canyons, and bays can be found to tuck away for extended periods of time if necessary.

Flooding is also a huge concern for many disaster scenarios. The necessity to abandon a BOV, cross a flooded road, and continue by foot toward your destination may be another reason to consider some type of small Bug Out Boat. A Bug Out Boat of some type, shape, or form may make sense for your situation. Before I discuss a few Bug Out Boat options, it is important to discuss some special equipment and needs that should be considered when evaluating Bugging Out, either entirely or partially, by water.

A portage may be necessary

Hidden jerry can fuel cache

BUG OUT BOAT SPECIAL CONSIDERATIONS

Boats present some special travel considerations and circumstances, regardless of the type of boat you use.

Portages/Locks

Should you decide to Bug Out via river, it's really important to know if there are portages along your intended route. Now is also a good time to research and locate any existing locks. Large locks may not be staffed and will consequently be impassible unless you can physically walk your boat around them. This fact alone may dictate the type of boat you choose or if it's practical to Bug Out via boat at all.

Power and Fuel

If you're considering an engine-powered boat, you'll need to also consider extra fuel and/or an extra solar-charging battery. Battery-powered trolling motors are excellent for pro-

pelling smaller craft and can also be carried around dams or locks. If you add a solar battery charger and extra battery you'll have a backup when the main battery gets low on juice, though this would be very limited as even a fully charged battery only lasts a handful of miles. Buried fuel caches in remote areas along the waterway can be a strategy for reducing pack weight and bulk. I would consider an extra oar or paddle a necessity for vessels small enough to paddle. However, if your BOL is downstream, then it's certainly possible to get there by current alone, Huck Finn style.

Security

Just as I recommended caltrops for land traveling vehicles in chapter eight, I would also recommend a prop-fouling device for traveling on water should another craft attempt to chase or follow you. I first heard of a prop-fouling device while watching the TV show *Whale Wars*. A prop fouler can be made by simply bunching together five to ten ½-inch (1cm) thick lengths (ten feet [3m] long) of floating rope (polypropylene rope floats). Tying them together at each end and in the middle creates two big sections of multiple net-like pockets that will bind an average boat prop when tossed in the path of a moving boat. The addition of a couple foam floats helps. Some crosscut sections from the cheap foam pool noodles work very well for this. I did test this to make sure it works. When I was a kid we had an old ski boat. I can remember on numerous occasions when the tow rope got twisted up and

BOV HIGHLIGHT: CHICAGO DUKW

VEHICLE MODEL: DUKW
MANUFACTURER: CHICAGO DUKW, WWW.DUKW.COM
PRICE: VARIES ON CONDITION

If you've ever been to the Wisconsin Dells, you've probably seen this type of vehicle in action while transporting tourists during amphibious sightseeing Duck Tours. The DUKW was designed for military use during WWII. It was a six-wheeled all-terrain vehicle used to transport troops across land, water and everything in between. It specialized in beach landings. Today, it's used primarily as a tourist vehicle to transport sightseers over streets, off-

road, and through rivers and lakes. A DUKW in good shape would be an incredible multi-environment Bug Out Vehicle/Boat. DUKWs were used as recently as Hurricane Katrina to navigate flood waters and rescue hurricane victims and have numerous other accounts of effective use during disaster scenarios.

DUKW

fouled the prop. This homemade version is basically the same concept.

Camo netting is the easiest way to camouflage a boat if a trip to shore is necessary. You'll be much more vulnerable to attack on shore than in open water.

Anchoring and Tying Down

An anchor with ample cordage will allow you to camp or rest in open water and should be considered. It can be difficult to maneuver a small boat to shore in fast currents, especially when trying to escape and evade or under stress. I have decided to pack a grappling hook and rope bag (550 Paracord) with my canoe. I can use this to toss ashore and pull myself in or as a quick and easy shore side anchor. This can also multipurpose for other Bug Out needs as well.

Food and Water Acquisition

When I'm hungry or thirsty in the wilderness, I head toward water. Not only can waterways be purified, filtered, or desalinated for drinking water but they are rich with food sources as well. A lightweight backpack filter is an essential piece of kit in your Bug Out Bag and can be used to gather drinking water from your fresh water liquid highway. Desalinators (devices that remove salt from salt water) are available in a variety

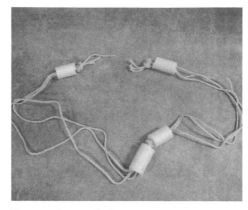
Homemade prop fouler

Prop fouler bound up in prop

Multifunction grappling hook

of sizes, from small backpack models to larger onboard units. These are pricey but essential if you're Bugging Out on the ocean or in brackish water. Solar stills are another option for converting salty or impure water into drinkable water. These have been used by the military for over forty years and can produce anywhere from one to four pints a day depending on sun exposure.

Pulling some trolling lines to catch fish while you travel is a way to extend food supplies should a Bug Out Journey last beyond the expected three days. A gill net is a much quicker way of catching ample fish (and bait). Also consider a small gaff for larger fish to prevent line breaks at the edge of the boat. A quiet bow-fishing rig would be a useful addition as well.

Insects

Mosquitoes, biting flies, and insects can be nearly debilitating along many waterways during certain times of the year. I know this from experience. The addition of some extra insect repellent and even heavy-duty bug nets to prevent unrelenting onslaughts will be much appreciated.

Wider Field of View

I rarely use my binoculars while hiking, but I regularly use them when canoeing and boating. I guess it's because the field of view is typically much longer when on water versus hiking through the woods. I can imagine that a good pair of binoculars will be a valuable asset during a waterway Bug Out to identify threats, navigate direction, and prepare for portages. While on the subject of navigation, a detailed map of all surrounding waterways is critical. This map should list all existing locks and dams, even if you have to hand draw them in yourself ahead of time while on a trial run.

Exposure to Sun

Sun protection is of utmost importance on open water. An awning, umbrella, sun hat, shemagh, sunglasses, and sunscreen are items that can help prevent sunburn. Severe sunburn can be a debilitating setback and first aid crisis.

Storage Options

Outfitting a boat with under-the-seat storage compartments not only keeps tools organized and out of sight but also extends storage capacity as well.

Aquatic Safety Devices

Water-specific tools and safety implements must also be considered. Life jackets, flares, air horns, and a bail bucket are all important emergency items. Sealing your gear in waterproof containers becomes of utmost priority when planning to travel by boat.

Launching Your Craft

I advise you preplan and have some boat launching sites/ramps in mind. Established boat ramps may be clogged, and it's a good idea to have a few backup locations in mind. You may have to carry some gear from your vehicle to the boat and you should plan for this. Anything larger than a paddle-power canoe or kayak will require a fairly clear launch site. You may have to clear small trees or branches in a pinch.

For all intents and purposes, boats can be divided into three main categories: human powered, sailboats, and motorboats. I have outlined the pros and cons of each below.

HUMAN POWERED: ROWBOATS, CANOES AND KAYAKS

Before you discount these small labor-intensive vessels as a BOV, consider the fact that individuals have navigated thousands of miles across entire oceans over the course of several months in almost every type of human-powered floating craft imaginable. It's amazing what's possible when you combine willpower and preparation.

An array of sun protection items: sunscreen, umbrella, hat and shemagh

Under-seat storage for boating-specific tools

Not an official boat ramp but will work just fine for many boats

Pros

Size: The size of most human-powered boats is both an advantage and disadvantage. The upside of being small is that most can be packed across land and portaged around dams, locks, and obstacles. They can also be piggybacked on top of other BOVs, such as trailers, trucks, SUVs, and cars to give an evacuee more options.

Flexible: Small lightweight boats can navigate thousands of miles of waterways, rivers, creeks, and lakes.

Fuel: Paddle power requires no fuel.

Discreet: These vessels are quiet, which is always a good thing when traveling through a potentially hostile environment.

Budget: Used canoes and kayaks can be found online to meet any budget. They are perfect candidates for bartering. You'd be surprised at what someone will trade for you to take that old canoe leaning up against the shed.

Maintenance: These small human-powered boats require little to no maintenance. They are EMP-proof and have virtually no mechanical parts. They can't get a flat tire either.

Water Levels: Small craft can still travel in just a few inches of water whereas larger boats will bottom out. River levels fluctuate and a drought could put a serious glitch in a Bug Out Boat plan.

Bug Out Old Town Canoe

Single-person kayak fitted with Bug Out Bag inside of 55-gallon trash bag with additional dry bags of supplies

Boats docked at marinas are ready to go at moment's notice

Ease of Launch: These boat options don't require specialized boat ramps or launch sites. Any reasonably accessible water edge will do just fine.

Cons

Power: You are the power. While paddling downstream is not that difficult, traveling upstream can be exhausting and nearly impossible in some instances. Make sure you're upstream of where you need to be.

Storage: These vessels aren't going to hold the same amount of supplies as a vehicle. In fact, they will be harder to navigate and even unstable when heavily loaded. You'll likely have to keep it light with just your Bug Out Bags and not much else.

Speed of Exit: Don't expect to win any races out of town. Waterways are rarely ever a direct route anywhere. If the disaster that's causing a Bug Out is immediately life threatening, the slow going of these paddle-powered boats may be a major concern.

SAILBOATS

In my opinion, sailboats represent one of the most interesting classes of BOVs. I have had students at Willow Haven who live more days out of the year on a sailboat than on land. In fact, many people live on sailboats year-round. A sailboat should be seriously considered if Bugging Out via a large body of water is in your plans. Even small sailboats (25 feet [7.6m] or less) can travel safely in the ocean while keeping close to shore. Sailing on rivers can be more difficult, especially those with fast currents and/or shallow depths. Sailing, more than any other type of boating, requires practice. I'd recommend keeping your boat in a slip at a marina. This way it's ready to go at a moment's notice. There may be a line at the boat ramp or weather conditions could make it difficult to launch. Trailering and launching sailboats can be tricky, especially larger ones with fixed keels.

Pros

Fuel: Sailboats are powered by the wind and can travel nearly infinite distances without fuel.

Storage: Larger boats with below-deck quarters can have ample storage room.

Extended Stay: While a BOV is for getting from point A to point B, many of the boats in this category allow for staying aboard with bunks, water storage tanks and purifiers, sinks, generators, and even bathrooms. This can certainly be an advantage in the event of an unfortunate setback.

Discreet: These vessels are quiet, which is always a good thing when traveling through a potentially hostile environment.

Food: With a few key fishing implements, access to food should not be an issue.

Water: Desalination/filtering/purifying will be necessary but drinking water should not be an issue if you plan ahead and have the necessary equipment.

Affordable: In contrast to what many may believe, used sailboats are very affordable. At the time of this writing, I found dozens of great sailboats on Craigslist locally (all with cabins, sinks, motors, toilets, and all rigging) for under five thousand dollars. A budget of ten to fifteen thousand dollars could buy a real gem.

Cons

Speed: Don't expect to win any speed records with a sailboat. They aren't very fast. In the sailing community, 10 mph (8.7 knots) is considered cruising along at an admirable clip. A distance of one hundred miles in a twenty-four hour time period is very respectable, even for fancy expensive rigs.

Security: Pirates aren't just in the movies. When it comes to security while out at sea or on a large body of water, you're pretty much on your own—especially in a Bug Out Scenario. A boat can be very vulnerable to security threats. Make sure you have a plan to respond to potential attacks.

Communications: Cell phones may work near shore but you'll quickly lose service when venturing into open water. Be sure to have the necessary communications equipment, such as marine radios, HAM radios, or satellite phones and the ability to power them.

Sea Sickness: Be sure to have medicines, such as Dramamine, to combat motion sickness among the crew.

Ease of Launch: Almost all of the boats in this category will require an accessible (and probably concrete) boat ramp. This fact may be limiting. Sailboats (especially those with fixed keels) can be tricky to launch. Some require long ramps with trailer tongue extensions or even a crane. Make sure you can launch your sailboat or always keep it at the marina ready to rock and roll.

Difficulty: Almost everything is more difficult and dangerous on open

HOLBOX/SHUTTERSTOCK.COM

Sailboat

Creek loading Bug Out Bags on pontoon

Speedboat with Bug Out Bags

water. Consequences of accidents and misfortunes are often greater and more complicated when on water than on land.

Special Considerations

- Keep a good patch kit for repairing ripped or damaged sails. Consider even keeping a backup sail on board.
- Don't forget extra fuel for the onboard motor and generator (if applicable).
- Consider a small dinghy just in case you can't dock at your destination for some reason. You may have to anchor in open water and transport supplies back and forth to land.

MOTORBOATS

From aluminum john boats with outboard motors to houseboats to pontoons to ski boats to multimillion-

dollar yachts, this category is as vast as the ocean itself. Regardless of what size craft or how much it costs, basic Bug Out Transport and Survival needs remain the same. These boats must be capable of getting people and survival supplies to a safe destination within a certain allotted amount of time.

One must be certain that the path of travel is clear and open, free of locks, dams, or other barricades that would require a portage. Most vessels in this category cannot be portaged due to weight and size. The inability to continue traveling by boat would require a Bug Out on foot. A detailed map (or maps) along the chosen waterway is critical just in case this happens.

No matter which style boat, a motor in peak condition is of the utmost importance. Paddling isn't an option for most of these boats. A second backup motor should be considered, especially if you are traveling far from shore. Ample fuel storage is critical. A small, last-ditch dinghy isn't a bad idea either for a variety of reasons.

A plan for launching the boat is also critical. If the boat is not kept at a slip, multiple boat launch sites should be identified and tested in advance. This should include at least one "unofficial" launch site just in case the others are jammed, damaged, or inaccessible.

Pros

Speed: Most motorboats have the advantage of speed with the exception of houseboats and pontoons.

Maneuverability: Many motorboats will have excellent maneuverability in open water.

Storage: You should have no problem fitting your Bug Out Supplies on most vessels in this category.

Extended Stay: While a BOV is for getting from point A to point B, many of the boats in this category allow for staying aboard with bunks, sinks, water storage tanks and purifiers, generators, and even bathrooms. This can certainly be an advantage in the event of an unfortunate setback.

Food: With a few key fishing implements, access to food should not be an issue.

Water: Desalination, filtering and purifying will be necessary but drinking water should not be an issue if you've planned ahead with the necessary equipment.

Cons

Ease of Launch: Almost all of the boats in this category will require an accessible (and probably concrete) boat ramp. This fact may be limiting.

Fuel: Motorboats aren't the most fuel-efficient means of travel. Pontoons, houseboats, and large motor powerboats are among the worst. Be sure to have ample fuel storage to make the trip. A practice trip made in advance is the best way to gauge fuel consumption, though wind and currents can cause significant discrepancies. Always overestimate fuel needs.

Discreet: These are among the louder vessels on the water. The noise from engines may draw unwanted attention.

Design: Most boats in this class are designed to be flashy, often including bright colored and/or metallic designs. Consider toning this down with a DIY spray-paint job or removable graphics.

Communications: Cell phones may work near shore, but you'll quickly lose service when venturing into open water. Be sure to have the necessary communications equipment, such as marine radios, HAM radios, or satellite phones.

Literally, a small house on a boat

Sea Sickness: Be sure to have medicines, such as Dramamine, to combat motion sickness among the crew.

SUMMARY

Bugging Out by boat certainly has a unique set of challenges but I'll admit the option is intriguing, and I also understand why many people I know have dedicated time and money to making this a viable Bug Out Strategy.

Over 80 percent of the Earth's surface is covered by water and flooding is commonplace in many disaster scenarios. Most people will find themselves crossing at least one bridge (probably many more) during a disaster evacuation. Water can be both a highway and a roadblock, depending on the options available. Something as simple as a canoe can open up a whole new world of possibilities to a survivor whose life depends on movement.

13 ▶ BUG OUT ATVS, UTVS, AND MOTORCYCLES

ATVS AND UTVS

I would need some convincing to choose an All-Terrain Vehicle (ATV) as a stand-alone Bug Out Vehicle, but I love the idea of piggybacking an ATV on a larger BOV such as a pickup truck or Bug Out Trailer. Regardless, ATVs certainly have advantages when it comes to getting off the beaten path and away from civilization. ATVs were invented to go places where traditional vehicles can't. The ATV movement started back in the 1960s.

Developments since then have created a class of vehicles that is mind-boggling in design, function, and capability. From multi-passenger, side-by-side utility vehicles (UTVs) to six-wheeled amphibious machines like the Argo, there is nowhere a disaster evacuee can't go. For those with the desire (and budget) to Bug Out from nearly any disaster imaginable,

an ATV or UTV of some sort is probably in the vehicle mix.

Access to and through unforgiving terrain isn't the only perk in this versatile class of machines. All have racks for strapping down gear and some even come equipped with mini truck-style beds for hauling bulky loads and stowing gear. Though miles per gallon of fuel depends on terrain, many ATVs can get over 30 mpg on open trails. One extra five-gallon tank can go a long way and is easily strapped on the corner of a spare rack.

One would prepare an ATV much like a traditional vehicle. Spare parts, off-road supplies, and fuel storage all apply. My old three-wheeler burns through the spark plugs like crazy. I never hit the trail without a few extras on hand and a tool kit to swap them out. ATV winches can be found for only a couple hundred dollars. Four-wheel drive ATVs are

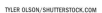

1980s Honda three-wheeler BOV

Snowmobile ATV Bug Out Convoy

Four-wheeler with cargo box mounted on back

Polaris UTV fitted with a Camoplast Tatou ATV/UTV T4S track system from www.atvtracks.net

preferred over the inferior two-wheel drive versions. A spare tire or patch kit is also a necessity. Twelve-volt power ports can be easily installed to run a small air compressor or to charge electronics, such as phones or radios, on the go.

Great little trailers can be found at lawn and garden stores. I use a molded plastic John Deere model designed for a lawn mower around the property at Willow Haven and it is unbelievable what a beating that thing has taken over the years. I have loaded it down with hundreds of pounds (kilograms) of rocks, wood, and tools with no ill effects. Gear storage is a major drawback of most ATVs and a small trailer is an easy way to drastically extend storage capacity.

ATV operators are traditionally "in open air" and exposed to the elements. Enclosed cabs are available for some ATVs but certainly not all

of them. Appropriate clothing, head wear, gloves, and shoes are critical when considering an ATV Bug Out, especially in four-season environments. Clothing to protect from underbrush and debris should also be considered. Whenever trail riding I always travel with a few N95 face masks to prevent from breathing in dust. This would certainly apply during a Bug Out with potential toxic ash as well. This list of pros and cons below may help to organize and prepare for Bugging Out on an ATV.

Pros

Off-Road: The off-road capabilities of most ATVs are staggering. They can go places traditional vehicles cannot. Many excel in rough terrain, mud, snow, sand, water, and steep slopes.

Maneuverability: ATVs are incredibly maneuverable both in congested traffic and in the woods. Many can even be moved or rotated by hand if necessary.

Fuel: Many ATVs get excellent gas mileage on open trails. This is significantly reduced in extreme off-road conditions.

Affordable: You can buy used ATVs for a few hundred dollars. I bought a good running Honda three-wheeler for 250 dollars. New models can cost as much as full-sized vehicles.

Patrol: ATVs make excellent patrol/recon vehicles while at a BOL or ahead of a convoy.

Maintenance: In general, ATVs are easier to work on than traditional vehicles.

Accessories: Many aftermarket accessories are available for ATVs. These range from storage boxes to gun racks. There is an accessory for almost every need.

BOV HIGHLIGHT: ARGO 8×8 750 HDI

VEHICLE MODEL: ARGO 8×8 750 HDI
MANUFACTURER: ONTARIO DRIVE & GEAR, WWW.ARGOATV.COM
PRICE: BASE SIX-WHEEL MODEL STARTS AT $9,995

PHOTO COURTESY OF ONTARIO DRIVE & GEAR

The Argo is a unique BOV option in a class all its own. Able to drive through dense brush, deep mud and snow, over rocks and logs and flooded areas, the Argo vehicles can go where no other off-road vehicle can go. Perhaps one of its most unique features is its amphibious capabilities. When the water gets too deep to drive through, the Argo floats like a boat and is able to continue through until solid ground is reached. Various accessories such as track kits, soft top, outboard motor mount, plus many more, all add to the versatility of these vehicles. When traveling through the harsh conditions disasters create, this vehicle gives a traveling survivor the option of going it on land or water!

Argo 8×8 750 HDi

KLR650 Dual Purpose Motorcycle from www.kawasaki.com

Ural Gear-Up from www.imz-ural.com

Cons

Storage: ATVs lack storage space. This can be extended with the addition of a trailer.

High Water: Most ATVs don't excel in fording deep water (except for the amphibious models like the Argo).

Exposure: Most ATV operators are exposed to the elements. Proper clothing and protective coverings for all Bug Out Supplies are imperative.

Noise: ATVs are not the most discreet vehicles available. Many ATV motors are loud and annoying, which can be a bad thing if trying to keep on the down-low.

Design: Most ATVs in this class are designed to be flashy, often including bright colored and/or metallic designs. Consider toning this down with a DIY spray-paint job or removable graphics.

Unstable: Some ATVs can be very unstable. I've flipped my three-wheeler more than once. Safety equipment, such as helmets, are a necessity.

Legality: Except a few geographic exceptions, ATVs aren't street legal. Driving ATVs on roads will elicit unwanted attention from authorities.

People: ATVs aren't ideal people haulers. Most only accommodate two comfortably. These are not an ideal solution for large families unless multiple units are in the budget.

EMP: All vehicles with electronic components are susceptible to Electromagnetic Pulse (EMP).

MOTORCYCLES, DIRT BIKES, AND SCOOTERS

A dual purpose/dual sport motorcycle like the classic Kawasaki KLR650 or the Ural Gear-Up is the ideal Bug Out Motorcycle. I'm also a big fan of the Yamaha TW200 Dual Sport bike. Road bike cruisers and choppers are worthless off the pavement and have the lowest ground clearance of all motorbikes. Dual purpose bikes handle just fine on pavement and perform equally as well on rugged dirt trails. Because they are designed for off-road travel, most have an impressive list of Bug Out-esque features, including higher ground clearance, knobby tires, larger fuel tanks, and rear fender racks. People adventure in remote places all over the globe using dual purpose bikes like the KLR650. Motorbikes aren't ideal for families (or even couples) but may be a perfect solution for a bachelor (or bachelorette) prepper who's hoping to get out of the city fast with just a Bug Out Bag and a few extra supply items. Those in congested, high-traffic cities will benefit from a motorbike's undeniable advantage navigating around

BOV HIGHLIGHT: TIM RALSTON SURVIVAL SERIES ROKON

VEHICLE MODEL: TIM RALSTON SURVIVAL SERIES ROKON
MANUFACTURER: ROKON, WWW.GEARUPCENTER.COM
PRICE: $7,935

ROKON® is the world's original and longest producing manufacturer of all-wheel drive American-made motorcycles. GearUp and ROKON have come together to produce a Tim Ralston Survival Signature Series Trail Breaker, specifically geared for the survival-minded set. It comes complete with camo package, front and rear game carriers and storage racks, rifle mount, .50 caliber ammo canister storage rigs, and hollow wheels for the transportation of extra fuel and water. For anyone seeking a motorcycle or ATV specifically designed as a BOV, the Ralston ROKON should get a hard look.

PHOTO COURTESY OF TIM RALSTON

Tim Ralston Survival Series ROKON

and through mass exodus traffic jams. Have you ever noticed that first responders on motorcycles are always the first on the scene in dense traffic accidents? Motorcycles will be the first out of a crowded disaster evacuation as well.

There's a reason why motorbikes are so popular in developing countries. They are affordable, reliable, easy to maintain, easy to troubleshoot, get great gas mileage, and are much more effective than four-wheeled vehicles on underdeveloped roads. It's also surprising how much a small motorbike can haul with a little creativity.

Purchased or homemade saddle bags can drastically extend a motorbike's storage capacity for luggage or extra fuel. For popular bikes like the KLR650 there are literally hundreds of aftermarket accessories to choose from. Customized bags are also made to fit over the gas tank and both wheels to further increase storage for long expedition-style trips. These make great storage areas for Bug Out Supplies as well.

Many may scoff at the mention of a scooter or moped as a potential BOV, but I'd sure love to have one as a backup if ever caught in traffic during a Bug Out when getting out of town was the difference between life and death. Thirty-five miles an hour

Overloaded Motorbike

Creek's Yamaha 50cc scooter with homemade egg crate storage boxes

Very unique Mountain Horse snow bike system from www.timbersled.com

on the road shoulder is a heck of a lot better than three miles an hour humping it with my 35-pound (16kg) BOB. I have an old Yamaha 50cc scooter and you wouldn't believe the places I've taken that bike. I've crossed creeks and fields, woven in and out of jammed traffic at rush hour, lifted it over fences, slid it under gates, and driven it through six inches of snow— all without a need for a license, title, or insurance. Is it my ideal BOV? No, but for a few hundred bucks used it sure makes a good backup. The gas mileage is second to none and for people who live in densely populated cities, storing a scooter is almost as easy as storing a bicycle. Some mopeds are pedal bikes and scooters rolled into one compact package.

Small trailers can easily be pulled by all motorbikes and even scooters. However, the addition of a trailer does nothing to protect the very exposed operator. Though a motorcycle makes a fast and small target for potential threats, exposure to the elements (weather and debris) is always a top survival priority and should be given the respect it warrants with weather-appropriate clothing and protective gear. Exposure is the number-one outdoor killer in the United States.

All of the same rules apply for motorbikes as they do for traditional vehicles when it comes to packing spare parts and a tool kit. Spare items, such as spark plugs, belts, chains, and tire patch kits along with the accompanying tools need to be figured into the available storage space. One may wish to purchase a common make/model of motorbike to ensure easier access to replacement parts. Parts for rare motorbikes will be nearly impossible to find during and after a crippling disaster.

Pros

Off-Road: There are few places on earth that motorcycles (excluding road bikes) can't go.

Maneuverability: Motorcycles, dirt bikes, and scooters are incredibly maneuverable both in congested traffic and in the woods. They can fit through extremely tight jams.

Size: Motorbikes are easy to store and conceal.

Fuel: Most motorbikes get excellent gas mileage. Many range in excess of 40 mpg. My scooter gets over 90 mpg.

Affordable: Used motorbikes are very affordable.

Patrol: Motorbikes make excellent patrol/recon vehicles while at a BOL or ahead of a convoy.

Maintenance: Motorcycles and scooters are easier to work on than traditional vehicles.

Escape and Evade: The speed and maneuverability of motorbikes make them ideal candidates for escape and evasion from potential threats.

Cons

Safety: Motorcycles require a certain level of proficiency, especially in aggressive off-road terrain. Safety equipment, such as helmets, is a necessity. Accidents are typically much more severe on motorbikes than in vehicles.

Exposure: All motorcycle operators are exposed to the elements. Proper clothing and protective coverings for any Bug Out Supplies is imperative.

Storage: Motorcycles lack storage space, though this can be extended with the addition of a trailer and strategically placed storage bags and boxes.

People: Motorcycles are not ideal for families.

Theft: Because of their size, motorbikes are more susceptible to theft.

EMP: All vehicles with electronic components are susceptible to EMP.

SUMMARY

Most ATVs and many motorcycles are designed specifically for getting through and to the places that normal vehicles can't. Consequently, they are a natural BOV choice when considering the potential harsh driving environments one may face. Further research will prove there are also important limitations such as protection from the environment and ability to carry gear. ATVs and motorbikes may be an ideal solution for a single person with a Bug Out Bag, but beyond that they may be better suited as an alternative piggyback BOV that rides in or on a larger vehicle. I do, however, love the idea of buzzing out of town on a dirt bike. The simplicity of that setup is very hard to deny.

14 > NON-ENGINE-POWERED BUG OUT VEHICLES

WITH ALL THE DISCUSSION OF EMP, (electromagnetic pulse), electronics, fuel types, gas mileage and other concerns that come with an engine-powered vehicle, I would be remiss not to discuss an entire class of BOVs to which none of that applies. A vast majority of the world's population uses vehicles that require no engine at all. While removing the engine component of a BOV presents an array of drawbacks, it also makes life a whole lot simpler—and cheaper. Below are some non-engine-powered BOVs to consider.

PEDAL-POWERED BIKES

Besides traditional four-wheeled vehicles, bicycles probably represent the second most popular BOV choice. As I mentioned in chapter two, the Yuba Mundo Cargo Bike (yubabikes.com) is part of my overall BOV mix. It is a Plan B piggyback vehicle that I keep in the back of my truck. I can travel farther faster and with more gear using this bike than I ever could on foot.

As roads and freeways turn into parking lots during mass exodus from densely populated cities, bicycles can cleanly, quietly, and swiftly weave in and out of traffic in search of safer ground ahead. They'll not need to stop for gas nor will a potential EMP affect them. Bicycles are affordable and extremely adaptable. Creativity is the limit when it comes to outfitting them. Panniers are available to store supplies, such as the ones seen on my Mundo bike. Inexpensive makeshift storage areas can be strapped on using anything from old egg crates to baskets. Bicycles can pull trailers and wagons loaded with supplies or even children and pets. Three-wheeled trikes are designed for stability and cargo hauling. On a recent trip to

Yuba Mundo Cargo Bike outfitted as Creek's Bug Out Bike

Bug Out Bag strapped to Bug Out Bike

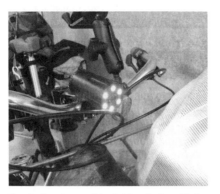

The Defender antitheft bicycle headlight from www.fortifiedbike.com

Smartphone X-Grip Mount from www.rammount.com

New York City, a friend and I hired a Trike-Taxi. Our driver was able to weave in and out of stopped traffic and deliver us to our destination much faster than the stop-and-go of a traditional cab. I couldn't help but think about how useful that trike would be for people who may want to escape a NYC Bug Out Scenario. I'm sure the price would go up!

Whether carrying cargo in developing nations or delivering ammunition on the battlefield during both World Wars, pedal bikes have endless uses and have been adapted to meet an infinite number of applications throughout history. The versatility and affordability of a bicycle makes it attractive to preppers from all walks of life. A reader of the Willow Haven blog recently e-mailed me a photo of his "Battle Bike" that he has prepared for a potential Bug Out. It's cleverly outfitted with a variety

of survival tools and spray-painted camouflage.

Maintenance and repair for a pedal-powered BOV is much less complicated than a motorized vehicle, especially the traditional four-wheeled kind. A simple set of hand tools, a tire patch kit, a hand pump, and a little creativity will get one through just about any mechanical malfunction.

Electric assist technology within the bicycle industry offers a unique element to pedal-powered travel. My Yuba Mundo Cargo Bike mentioned earlier has an electric conversion-ready frame to add an optional electric assist module. The Optibike from www.gearupcenter.com is another example of electric-hybrid bicycle technology. Electric-assisted technology not only helps with steep climbs and heavy loads, but can also help you travel farther faster. Some even recharge the

Sample bicycle repair kit with multi-wrench, patch kit, Slime Tire Sealant, and hand pump

Ty "The Leftcoastist" Gladden's Battle Bike

batteries while the operator pedals. Universal, bolt-on, gas-powered bicycle motor kits are also available for a couple hundred dollars online. These can convert almost any standard bicycle into a hybrid motorbike that travels speeds in excess of 30 mph.

Like with motorcycles and ATVs, exposure is a primary concern when considering a Bug Out Bike. Riding these during inclement weather quickly becomes an issue. Certain terrain, such as mud and snow, are nearly impassible and drastically reduce the practicality of bicycle travel. Weather-appropriate clothing and storage containers are imperative.

Pros

Size: Bicycles are easier to store, transport, and maneuver.

Flexible: Bicycles can travel on a huge variety of terrains.

Fuel: No fuel required other than water and food for the operator.

Discreet: Bicycles are quiet and inconspicuous. One can travel discretely through populated areas and not draw attention. They are also easier to hide and camouflage than larger BOVs.

Budget: Bicycles (especially used) are very affordable. They are also not expensive to accessorize. "Spare part" bikes can be purchased for just a few dollars at almost any garage sale.

License and Insurance: No paperwork, license, or insurance is required to operate a bicycle.

Maintenance: Bicycles are much easier to repair and maintain than traditional vehicles. A small tool kit, tire patch kit, and hand pump sums up a field maintenance kit. Parts are also readily accessible around every corner.

Bug Out Horse

Bug Out Camels

Family: Trailers can be purchased to tote small children, gear, and pets.

EMP: Non-issue.

Cons

Power: The operator is the power. One's physical condition has a large influence on speed and distance of travel.

Storage: Bicycles have limited storage capacity.

Speed of Exit: Don't expect to win any races out of town. Average speed will be around 7–12 mph.

Exposure: Exposure to weather, environmental conditions, predators, and people is extremely high.

HORSES AND OTHER BUG OUT ANIMALS

The original all-terrain vehicles weren't vehicles at all. They were animals, primarily equines. Man has been using animals many, many times longer than mechanical vehicles to trans-

port themselves and their gear from point A to point B. In fact, the word "horsepower" associated with modern engines has roots in the comparison of engines during the eighteenth century to the power of draft horses. Whether riding camels through the sands of Arabia or a donkey through a rugged pass in the Rocky Mountains, animals are the original BOVs. It's always hard to beat the original.

Animals make excellent But Out Vehicles in three respects. They can be ridden, they can carry gear, or they can pull some sort of a wagon, sled, or cart with people and/or gear inside. Either way, a huge variety of animals excel in these tasks. Below are a few examples of animal-powered Bug Out Vehicles:

- horse with/without a buggy
- goat with saddlebags or pulling a cart
- large working dog with saddle bags or pulling a cart

Large-breed dog fitted with doggy backpacks

Goat pulling small wagon that could be used in a Bug Out Situation

- dogs pulling a snow sled
- lama fitted with canvas panniers
- donkeys and mules carrying gear behind a horse (pack mule)

One of the major drawbacks to using large animals, such as horses, for BOV is they must be kept and cared for in advance of (and during) a potential Bug Out. These are living beings that must be fed, watered, exercised, and looked after nearly around the clock. This isn't practical for the majority of households. Keeping large animals takes space, time, and money. However, many overlook that large working-breed dogs such as Labradors, rottweilers, mastiffs, Great Danes, shepherds, and huskies can contribute substantially to an on-foot Bug Out. These dogs are bred to work and excel when their instincts and breeding can be put to

good use. They *want* to work hard! With a little training, working-breed dogs can comfortably pull a wagon, sled, or cart carrying Bug Out Bags, supplies, or small children. And, they will enjoy doing it! Huskies and trained reindeer still pull sleds in northern climates all over the globe. In the Alaskan Iditarod dog sled race, an average of sixteen dogs pull a sled over one thousand miles in just under two weeks. Many animals have an amazing potential to contribute during Bug Out conditions. Small farm animals, like goats and ponies, can also be trained to pull carts, wagons, and sleds as well.

Animals require repair and maintenance kits as well, except these look much more like what's in our own Bug Out Bags than in a tool kit. At a minimum, animals will require food, water, feeding/watering containers, and first aid supplies. Some may require prescription medication. Appropriate leashes, muzzles, halters, leads, crates, blankets, saddles, and riggings must also be considered. In addition, owners should have up-to-date shot records for animals as well, especially dogs. Documentation may be required for entry into certain zones, shelters, or areas.

Animals need to be trained in advance! Don't expect anything to go smoothly if a dog's first time pulling a wagon is during a real-life Bug Out. If a working animal isn't regularly worked before a Bug Out, don't expect it to perform well under pressure either. It needs practice just as we need practice. How do your animals respond when a gun is fired? Do they run? Jump? Bite? How does your animal react to traffic? Honking horns? Crowds of people? Make sure you prepare your animal for any possible Bug Out Scenario just as you would the other members in your family.

Pros

Fuel: Working animals do not require traditional petro-based fuel.

All-terrain: Animals are all-terrain travelers and can go places that motorized vehicles (even ATVs) only dream of.

Companionship: Animals give friendship and companionship in bleak and depressing times.

Noise: Animals can travel in near silence.

Repair and Maintenance: Mechanical skills are not required to operate an animal. However, animal husbandry skills are important.

Storage: Some animals, such as horses and mules, can pack up to 20 percent of their body weight in gear. That's a lot of Bug Out Supplies.

EMP: Non-issue.

Warmth: Animals can also provide warmth on a cold night. This concept is where the phrase "three dog night" originates.

Cons

Advance Prep: Keeping a Bug Out Animal is much different than storing an ATV or bicycle. Animals require space, water, food, time, and protection. They certainly do not fit into some lifestyles.

Food/Water: Though animals don't require gasoline to run, they do require food and water. If these items can't be sourced along the Bug Out Route, they must be packed and brought along.

Exposure: The operator (and gear) is highly exposed when riding or leading animals.

Speed: Animals don't have the speed or stamina of motorized vehicles.

Storage: While large animals can carry much more gear than humans, their storage capacity is very limited as compared to vehicles.

CARTS, WAGONS, AND STROLLERS

Photos were captured during the Hurricane Katrina evacuation of victims pulling supplies along the roadways in everything from large wheeled trash barrels to shopping carts and travel luggage. They were desperate for something to help carry additional supplies as they sought safety beyond the reach of flood waters.

Creek pulling converted deer cart from www.sportsmansguide.com

Handcart

A handcart has always been a part of my personal Bug Out Plan. My deer cart from www.sportsmansguide.com allows me to pull a wide variety of extra supplies with surprisingly little effort, especially along paved roads. It's designed to haul a dead deer out of the woods and I've comfortably pulled 150-plus pounds (68-plus kg) on a paved path near my home for over five miles. Using two climbing carabiners I can hitch this to the back of my belt or the frame of my backpack and pull it like a trailer behind me. I've found this to be more comfortable than pulling it by hand. It also folds nearly flat for easy storage. This cart is my last-ditch option before continuing an evacuation with just my Bug Out Bag. My solution before this cart was a four-wheeled wagon from my local

Poor choices of Bug Out Handcarts

Trans-Port-RRR Big Game Cart by www.loomansoutdoor.com

lawn and garden store. Wheeled Bug Out Carts allow evacuees to carry additional supplies beyond what three-day Bug Out Bags may be able to contain. For many like myself, carts aren't necessary. For some, it is impossible to continue a Bug Out Journey on foot without one.

It's not realistic for families with small children to travel on foot for an extended period of time without some assistance. This is even difficult on the paved streets of Disney World with fanny packs, let alone loaded down with Bug Out Bags in the midst of a disaster evacuation. Infants and small children must be carried and/or wheeled in some kind of stroller, cart, or wagon. Carrying them and the Bug Out Supplies in your arms or on your back isn't practical.

Those with small children aren't the only ones who can benefit from wheeled carts. For some, pulling a cart with a Bug Out Bag is easier than carrying the pack on their back.

BOV HIGHLIGHT: EXODUS EMERGENCY EVACUATION CART

VEHICLE MODEL: EXODUS EMERGENCY EVACU-
ATION CART
MANUFACTURER: EXODUS DISASTER
PREPAREDNESS & EVACUATION CART,
WWW.EXODUSSOLUTIONS.NET
PRICE: $2,990 (STANDARD MODEL)

The Exodus Emergency Evacuation Cart by EXODUS Solutions was designed and manufactured with disaster evacuation in mind. This handcart has urethane foam no-flat tire, heavy-gauge solid aluminum construction, twenty-eight liters of water storage, and even brakes. It even has a weapons bay and MOLLE (Modular Lightweight Load-carrying Equipment) compatible side panels. Check out this unique BOV solution on their website.

EXODUS Emergency Evacuation Cart

Nimble Cargo Scooter from nimblescooters.com

Jogging stroller

Some people just aren't able to physically carry a 30-plus-pound (13-plus kg) backpack for long distances due to a variety of physical conditions or limitations. With a little creativity, a harness can be rigged so a cart or wagon can be pulled from the waist. This can help to further reduce stress on the arms and wrists. I rigged a similar harness to pull my deer cart as a trailer behind my cargo bike with two large climbing carabiners. As I've mentioned, it can also be rigged to my belt or backpack as well. An external ALICE pack frame can be purchased online or at an Army/Navy surplus store for just a few dollars and would work great as a stand-alone cart/wagon harness anchor point.

Push Scooters

I have a friend who keeps a Razor scooter in the trunk of his car as a po-tential Get Home Vehicle in the event of an unforeseen breakdown or traffic jam. Even push scooters, skateboards, and long boards are better than walking. The Nimble Cargo Scooter from nimblescooters.com has an innovative cargo box to stow a Bug Out Bag or additional supplies. A simple BOV like this has many advantages over traveling by foot in an urban concrete jungle and along congested paved roads. These types of vehicles can easily stow in a BOV, coat closet, or under the desk at work. Think outside of the BOV box!

Strollers

Some baby strollers have evolved into rugged trail-runner models for busy moms and dads who want to continue jogging and strolling with their small children. These off-road type strollers make perfect solutions

191

Landscape wagon modified as Bug Out Wagon

for toting children or just supplies alone. I have a friend who has a Bug Out Stroller. He is single and doesn't have children but he does have a cabbage-patch style baby doll toy stuffed with 15 pounds (7kg) of 9mm ammunition cradled inside the bassinet. He also has a shotgun wrapped in a baby blanket mounted to the side of the stroller, which is on a swivel and can pivot up at a moment's notice. His Bug Out Bag is a big diaper bag. I know this sounds ridiculous, but he claims the strategy is to look less threatening because he has a baby in a stroller. I'm not 100 percent convinced either way, but I have to give him credit for creativity! It certainly is an urban camouflage strategy.

While at the mall not too long ago I saw a woman pushing a stroller with four kids in it! It was like pushing a mini set of gymnasium bleachers but

I suppose it is at least an option on paved roads for families with multiple young children. Having multiple young children presents a unique set of challenges, especially when having to travel by foot. Multiple seat strollers do exist but I suspect they would only be practical on paved roads and trails.

Wagons

Wagons are another excellent solution, but I will report from personal experience that these (even pneumatic tire versions) are best used on pavement. The landscape wagon I had prior to the deer cart doesn't pull nearly as well through heavy grass, wooded environments, and even loose gravel. However, it works very well on paved roads and packed trails. It also does not break down flat like my deer cart. The Radio Flyer type wagons are definitely limited to paved travel. Their tires rut very quickly in grass, mud, leaves, forest debris, and sand.

Tie-downs, bungee cords (looprope.com), and ratcheting straps have all been necessary while trying to secure bulky loads on each of the Bug Out Carts I've experimented with over the years. Like all aspects of Bug Out Training, it's important to practice strapping on the Bug Out Bags and gear to a cart in advance. These trial runs help to determine exactly what types and how many straps one will need. I've found that minor shifting of gear during travel makes using standard rope very difficult.

Pros

Affordable: Most Bug Out Carts are extremely affordable.

Children: Bug Out Carts are a great solution for evacuating on foot with infants and small children.

Flexible: Most Bug Out Carts can be drug through and pushed over a large diversity of terrain including rocks, wooded areas, creeks, streams, meadows, and trails.

Pets/Animals: Large-breed dogs and farm animals can be trained to pull carts and wagons. In contrast, these wagons can also help carry smaller lap dogs or elderly pets that may not be able to keep up on foot.

Fuel: Carts do not require fuel.

Stealth: Carts and wagons are very quiet and do not draw unwanted noise attention.

Camouflage: Carts are much easier to hide and camouflage than larger vehicles.

Cons

Speed: Speed of exit is limited to how fast one can walk.

Power: Carts and wagons must be pulled or pushed. Certain terrain, such as steep climbs, marshes, and sand, can be very limiting and exhausting.

Fitness: Trust me, one must be practiced and in good shape to pull any kind of wagon or handcart even just a few miles on paved road. Your physical strength will limit the amount of gear you can haul.

SUMMARY

I can't stress the importance of taking a mock Bug Out Hike. This simple exercise will tell you so much about your Bug Out Bags, your carts or wagons, and your own ability to haul them. I have made countless adjustments to my pack and cart setup based upon mock Bug Out Hikes. Trust me, you don't have to hike all the way to your Bug Out Location to discover areas of improvement. Insufficiencies and problems will present themselves very quickly. These are the times to work out the kinks in a plan. During a Bug Out, it's too late.

Non-motorized vehicles are ideal backup BOVs for a variety of reasons. They are typically very affordable. They are also very plentiful. Smaller footprints make it reasonable to piggyback them onto or into primary BOVs without much effort. What they lack in storage capacity, speed, and power they make up for in price, maintenance costs (time and money) and simplicity of operation.

BOV AIRPLANES AND EXPERIMENTAL AIRCRAFT

WE'VE DISCUSSED LAND TRAVEL and water travel. For some, taking flight might be an ideal escape from ground zero. Air travel is no longer reserved for the uber-wealthy. Small experimental flying machines are available for just a few thousand dollars. If weather permits, evacuating as the crow flies could be the fastest way out of Dodge.

However, unless one has made arrangements to launch a flying BOV directly from a backyard landing strip (or similar), this strategy must also involve a vehicle to transport one to the takeoff location. This, combined with the obvious drawbacks, including weather conditions and operation expertise makes choosing a flying BOV a very complicated decision. The extreme advantages are countered by extreme challenges and risks. Personally, when planning for a potential Bug Out, my strategy is to eliminate as much risk as possible. Choosing an aircraft of any kind as a primary BOV is just too risky for me. This is certainly not to say that it cannot be done and also not to say that it doesn't make a good additional BOV option for those with the means to do so.

AIRPLANES

From private luxury jets to smaller bush planes, taking to the sky certainly has its advantages. I'm surprised each year at the number of pilots who fly to my courses in Indiana from out of state and land at a small airport nearby rather than drive. Fractional and shared ownership of planes makes piloting much more affordable and practical than owning a plane outright. A lot of pilots are just average Joes who build their own aircraft from kits for around the price of a traditional car. Gone are the days of needing a million dollars to own a plane. A Sport Pilot License can be earned by a seventeen-year-old with as little as twenty hours of training.

I'm reminded of several great survival movies (and even a Stephen King novel) where those with access to a plane were the only ones who made it out alive. Flying over clogged expressways or ground-level disasters could very well be a reality for some who own a Bug Out Plane. Short takeoff and landing (STOL) bush planes, like the Backcountry Super Cub, can land and take off in an insanely short distance on rugged terrain. Some nearly fly straight up like a helicopter. This allows for a tight takeoff in less-than-perfect conditions and a remote landing at a predetermined Bug Out Location far from urban reach. Backcountry planes can also be fitted with pontoons for water landings or skis for snow and ice landings. Is your BOL located on a remote backcountry lake? No problem! Planes offer a very unique solution to Bug Out travel.

Just as one traveling by vehicle should have a paper map and compass as a backup to electronic navigation, pilots should have a backup plan as well. This should include a series of landmarks chosen ahead of time that can help navigate to a Bug Out Landing Strip. It's also important to identify several possible landing areas along the route, just in case an emergency landing is required.

Pros

Travel Speed: Even small backcountry planes can cruise in excess of 120 mph. The Cessna Citation X can cruise at speeds up to 604 mph. Couple these speeds with straight-line travel and one can get from point A to B really fast.

Speed Away From Disaster: Assuming one can get to the plane and take off, the speed away from ground zero beats nearly any other BOV option.

Takeoff: Some backcountry bush planes can be in the air faster than most muscle cars can go from 0-60 mph. These short takeoff and landing (STOL) aircraft can easily land in remote Bug Out Locations and are designed specifically to do so.

Terrain: Some planes can be fitted with pontoons for water takeoffs/landings, skis for snow and ice takeoffs/landings, and large tundra wheels for uneven or sandy takeoffs/landings.

Avoid the Crowds: The sky will certainly be less crowded than the paved roads out of town.

Cons

Storage: Some smaller planes lack storage space, especially when it comes to extra passengers.

Fuel: Refueling could be nearly impossible during a large-scale chaotic disaster. Consider extra fuel storage on board the aircraft. A plane that uses auto gas versus aviation gas may be advantageous due to availability.

Weather: A Bug Out Plane could be completely useless if bad weather is the reason for a Bug Out.

Budget: Airplanes are an expensive BOV, regardless of which one you choose. They are expensive to purchase, store, maintain, and operate.

No-Fly Orders: It's not uncommon during large-scale disasters, especially terrorist related, for the government to issue a regional or national "no-fly" order. Disobeying the order could result in severe consequences, including an F-16 on your tail.

Maintenance: Airplanes should be meticulously maintained after each and every use.

Airplane Bug Out

Float plane

License: A pilot's license is required to fly. This takes significant time and money to acquire.

Navigation: GPS may not be available. Be sure to have a series of visible landmarks chosen in advance to help guide you to a Bug Out Landing Strip.

Weight: All airplanes have weight limits for cargo. Be sure to know what they are. Cargo nets and ratchet straps should also be considered in order to keep cargo from shifting during flight.

Airport: Consider keeping the plane in smaller privately owned hangers and airports. It is likely that authorities will quickly shut down larger airports or that they will be a logistical nightmare to mitigate.

Noise: Landing in a remote airstrip may draw unwanted attention.

HELICOPTERS AND GYROCOPTERS

Helicopters and gyrocopters are unique in that they can get in and out of places where all other aircraft cannot. This is why most rescue operations and special ops teams use helicopters exclusively. Maneuverability in the air is also unparalleled.

VISUAL FLIGHT RULES

In the event of a complete collapse, it's not hard to imagine the absence of GPS navigation, landing beacons, radar, or ground communications from Air Traffic Control. It is important for pilots to understand and abide by basic Visual Flight Rules (VFR), including flight altitude. In cases of limited visibility and poor communications, landings and takeoffs can become a deadly game of Russian roulette.

Helicopters provide a quick escape

Creek flying a powered paraglider over Gulf of Mexico

If weather permits, I cannot think of a faster and more direct way out of a crowded city than by helicopter. Helicopters can deliver people and goods to extremely remote Bug Out Locations that may not be accessible by any other vehicle or even by foot.

Pros

Takeoff and Landing: Helicopters can take off and land in very small areas.

Speed: Helicopters and many gyrocopters are very fast as compared to traveling by vehicle on land or water.

Maneuverability: Helicopters have the unique ability to maneuver within areas other aircraft cannot, such as tall buildings, forests, and mountains.

Cons

Training: Requires extensive training to operate.

License: A license is required to fly helicopters and gyrocopters.

Budget: Helicopters and gyrocopters are expensive to purchase, store, maintain, and operate.

Crash Landing: Helicopter emergency landings are incredibly dangerous.

Storage: Small helicopters and especially gyrocopters have very limited storage space.

No-Fly Orders: It's not uncommon during large-scale disasters, especially terrorist related, for the government to issue a regional or national "no-fly" order. Disobeying the order could result in severe consequences, including an F-16 on your tail.

Maintenance: Helicopters and gyrocopters should be meticulously maintained after each and every use.

Navigation: GPS may not be available. Be sure to have a series of visible

Larger trike-mounted powered paraglider

Motorized hang glider

landmarks chosen in advance to help guide you to a Bug Out Landing Strip.

Weight: All helicopters and gyro-copters have weight limits for cargo. Be sure to know what they are. Cargo nets and ratchet straps should also be considered in order to keep cargo from shifting during flight.

Airport: It is likely that authorities will quickly shut down larger airports or that they will be a logistical nightmare to mitigate. A smaller, privately owned hanger and airport is a better choice.

Noise: Landing in a remote area may draw unwanted attention.

SINGLE-MANNED AND EXPERIMENTAL AIRCRAFT

Most aircraft in this category are very sensitive when it comes to flying conditions and weather. I own a backpack-style powered paraglider. The photo above is of me flying over the ocean off the coast of Florida. In near perfect weather conditions, I suppose I could load a few extra survival supplies on board, but most of these smaller, single-manned flying machines are designed for recreational piloting. My paraglider requires no license to operate and costs less than most ATVs. Larger trike units are better equipped to carry more gear and even passengers.

Small experimental aircraft have been used by military forces across the globe for stealthily placing soldiers into strategic locations. Even hot-air balloons have been used to silently spy on enemy forces and drop bombs. Many of these types of units are much quieter than full-size airplanes. They also require much less training. In most cases a person can be flying with less than a day of training. These include a vast array of lightweight and low-profile flying machines.

Pros

Affordable: Experimental-type flying machines are very affordable, often costing less than an ATV.

Quiet: Many flying units in this class are much quieter than anything else that will carry someone through the sky. I can fly 300 feet over a picnic and not disturb anyone.

Training: Little training is required to fly most craft in this category.

License: Many flying machines in this category do not require a pilot's license to operate.

Takeoff and Landing: Takeoff and landing distances can be very small. I can leave the ground with my paraglider in two steps during ideal wind conditions.

Cons

Speed: Most small, single-manned alternative aircraft are not fast. My paraglider, for example, tops out at 30 mph while traveling with the wind.

Distance: Fuel tanks are small and thus flying time is limited is one to three hours in most cases.

Danger: These units can be dangerous to fly, especially in high winds and unstable weather conditions.

SUMMARY

As with non-motorized vehicles, I see flying BOVs as an alternative backup to Plan A. A flying BOV certainly gives an evacuee more options and I am a guy who likes options. However, this option comes with a price in both cost of ownership and training. My best advice is to buy an airplane because you've always dreamed of being a pilot. Then, the bonus is that you may one day use it as a BOV. I don't think I can make the argument to buy a flying BOV for the sole purpose of Bugging Out. It's just not that practical for most lifestyles and disaster scenarios.

16 ▶ THE BUG OUT PLAN

BUILDING A BUG OUT VEHICLE is one component of a larger overall Bug Out Plan. It is simply a means to get you, your loved ones, and your survival supplies from ground zero to a safer destination. It's important to divide and conquer when it comes to constructing a well strategized Bug Out Plan. Your BOV is a very important, but is only one element in a four-part plan.

THE BUG OUT PLAN

A Bug Out Plan or BOP is your overall action plan should a real Bug Out actually be necessary. It is a pre-thought out play-by-play guidebook to getting out of Dodge. It can be as simple as a checklist or checklists (for families). Preparing and storing a Bug Out Bag is a part of your overall BOP. There are many facets to consider before, during, and after a Bug Out. Below are a few important questions that should be covered in a BOP.

- Where is the family/team meeting?
- What vehicle will we be driving?
- What needs to be done to the house to prepare it for an evacuation?
  - Water- and fireproof safe installed
  - Lock away valuables
  - Turn off water and utilities
  - Plug drains
  - Disconnect gas lines
  - Secure doorways
  - Leave notes
  - Extra gas cans
- Who is responsible for each task?
- Does each person have a checklist of responsibilities?
- Are any pets going?
- If we Bug Out, where is our destination?
- How will we be getting there?

A disaster Bug Out is going to be mass chaos! Having an action plan will expedite the process as well as help to avoid costly mistakes. Don't think you can possibly remember to do everything without a clear and concise checklist and action plan. This plan is your Bug Out Plan.

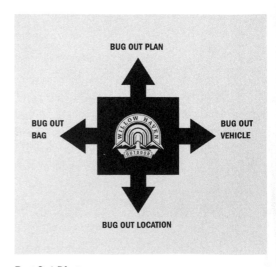

Bug Out Diagram

The Bug Out Bag, a 72-hour disaster survival kit

Be prepared to evacuate on foot

BUG OUT BAG

If you're reading this book then chances are you are already familiar with the phrase Bug Out Bag. You may have even read my book titled *Build the Perfect Bug Out Bag,* which has become the go-to guide for those looking to build a 72-hour disaster survival kit.

A Bug Out Bag is a backpack that contains all of the survival supplies that you and your family may need if forced to evacuate your home due to a large-scale disaster. As I've mentioned previously, traveling by vehicle is a luxury and not a guarantee. A Bug Out Bag is designed to be carried on foot if necessary. Below, I briefly describe the different considerations and supply categories that should be considered when building your 72-hour Bug Out Bag. My book on this subject elaborates on each component in great detail and provides suggested products, survival tips, additional resources, and at-home exercises.

The Pack

A Bug Out Bag should be a backpack that allows for hands-free travel. Backpacks are easier to carry over long distances and help distribute heavy loads evenly on the back, shoulders, and hips. It should be comfortable and compartmentalized. Consider packs that are "average" looking in earth tone colors so as to not stick out in a crowd and garner unwanted attention.

Shelter

Exposure to the elements is the number-one outdoor killer in the United States. More people die in the outdoors of exposure than any other cause. In extreme conditions, humans can survive only three hours without shelter. Weather-appropriate clothing is our first shelter defense from Mother Nature. God gave us brains not fur, so plan ahead by packing the necessary gear in a Bug Out Bag. In addition to seasonal clothing items, a Bug Out Bag should contain at least one survival shelter solution such as a lightweight backpacking tent. Redundant "backup" shelters are also a good idea. These could include a tarp, poncho, and emergency survival blanket.

Water

Our bodies are more than 70 percent water. Every bodily function depends on proper hydration. Dehydration leads to poor decisions, cramping, dizziness, and ultimately organ failure. Every Bug Out Bag should not only contain three days of fresh drinking water but also tools in which to source, filter, and purify more. Items such as water filters and purification tablets are essential to every well-prepared kit.

RAIN PONCHO

The military-style rain poncho is a great multipurpose item. It can be used as an emergency survival shelter. Here are three different configurations that I've used:

Poncho ridge line lean-to

Poncho tent

Poncho diagonal lean-to

Pump filter system

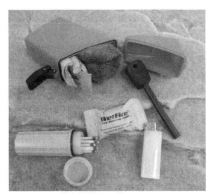

Sample Bug Out Bag fire kit

Fire

Fire is integrally related to almost every basic human survival need. It can help regulate core body temperature and stave off hypothermia, boil and purify open-sourced water, cook and warm food, provide light in nighttime and low-light conditions, offer companionship, signal for rescue, and even keep wild predators at bay. Every survival kit should have at least two fire components: ignition source and fire tinder. With these two items, one has an almost guaranteed way to make fire should it be necessary.

Food

Although we can live approximately three weeks without food, most people don't react too well to skipping meals. Moodiness is soon followed by dizziness and light-headedness, which leads to slow progress and less-than-perfect decisions. High-calorie bars make perfect open-and-eat Bug Out Meals that require no preparation. These also have a long shelflife. Keep it simple when it comes to food.

First Aid

Disaster creates less-than-safe travel environments and it's not hard to imagine the need for basic first aid supplies. A first aid kit stocked with a variety of bandages, tapes, and pads to accommodate the unexpected emergency is essential.

Self Defense

Violent crime spikes in the midst of every disaster. Criminal-minded individuals and gangs use the cloak of chaos and darkness to further exploit disaster victims. Self-defense tools become very important in a time when first responders and authority figures can't be in all places at all times. A BOB should include items for self-defense.

Pepper spray secured to Bug Out Bag shoulder strap

Cutting fence with multitool wire cutters

Hands-free headlamp

Hygiene

Personal hygiene is imperative during times when public services such as electricity, water, and trash removal are off-grid. Antibacterial wipes, trash bags, and a personal hygiene kit can help keep sickness and infection at bay.

Tools

Survival tools such as a knife and multitool have hundreds of uses to a survivor traveling through a disaster zone. From cutting rope and food preparation to processing firewood and self-defense, the uses for basic survival tools are endless. Other tools can include a small saw, hatchet, machete, or folding shovel.

Lighting

Traveling during dark or low light conditions can be dangerous for a variety of reasons. A hands-free headlamp or small flashlight is necessary to set up camp after dusk or to navigate through dark off-grid buildings. Flashlights can also be used as signaling tools.

Communications

Keeping abreast of disaster-related information is critical while evacuating. A hand-crank emergency radio with NOAA Weather Band can receive emergency information even if

Hand-crank emergency radio

Important documents in waterproof map case

batteries or AC power isn't available. A pen and paper can also be used to record important information such as directions and phone numbers. Cell phone service is almost always affected during large-scale disasters. High call volume can quickly overwhelm cell tower capabilities. Text messages may be the best form of post-disaster communication. Some extra cash stashed in a BOB is never a bad idea just in case power outages make credit card terminals or ATMs non-operational.

Important Documents

Copies of important documents such as insurance paperwork, bank information, marriage certificates, and pet vaccination records should be kept in a waterproof folder and ready to stash into a BOB at a moment's notice. In the event of critical damage to the home, having these documents all in one place while traveling makes putting your life back together much less complicated.

I believe that building a Bug Out Bag is the best and most logical first step in preparing for potential large-scale disasters. My mantra has always been "It's not *if* but *when*," and have a pre-prepared kit ready to grab at any given moment could be the competitive edge one needs to make it out alive!

BUG OUT LOCATION

How can you expect to get there if you don't know where you are going? A Bug Out Location or BOL is your destination point. This could be your home away from home for quite a while so it needs to be chosen with thoughtful consideration. Below are my basic guidelines about a BOL:

Realistic Distance

It is my opinion that a BOL needs to be at least one gas tank away from all large cities. Should there be a large-scale economic, infrastructure and supply chain collapse, people will be venturing out from the cities into the surrounding area in search of resources such as food, fuel, medicines, etc. If this happens, fuel will be scarce and very costly. Being at least one gas tank away will drastically limit much of this activity.

At the same time, a BOL needs to be within a 72-hour walk from your home. If for some crazy reason you need to abandon your vehicle, you should be able to reach your BOL on foot within the survival time frame of your Bug Out Bag—72 hours. My BOL is eighty miles away from my home. I really hope I never have to walk eighty miles with my BOB.

House, Hotel, Woods, Where?

I believe your BOL should be the home of a friend or family member who has agreed to house you and your family in the event of a Bug Out. You can offer them the same exchange. I'm not a big fan of Bugging Out to a hotel simply because you have no guarantees of availability. I've also heard more times than I can count from friends within the survivalist community about their plans to Bug

Out into the wilderness. Typically, whoever says this hasn't spent much time in the woods. Surviving for an extended period of time in a wilderness environment is extremely difficult, especially after you've exhausted your immediate Bug Out Supplies. Bugging Out into the primitive wilderness is not practical or realistic. It sounds fun and adventurous but the reality of it is quite the opposite—even for an experienced survivalist. My BOL is my childhood home, my parents' farm in southern Indiana. It is important to make BOL arrangements in advance. Here are a few short-term BOL options to consider:

- stay with friends or family (preferred option)
- purchase and prepare a small plot of land with a camper, travel trailer or cabin

ISTOCK.COM/© CONSTANT GARDENER

Remote Cabin

Two of six supply shelves at Creek's BOL

Wood-burning stove, solar power kit, candles, and oil lamp

- stay mobile in an RV
- stay at campgrounds/parks/retreat centers
- establish relationships with local/regional preppers through clubs and meetings
- network with friends, coworkers, and church members
- have a second home (not necessarily short term)

Should I have supplies at my BOL?

Yes, you should. I keep a three-month food storage supply at my BOL as well as an extensive first aid kit. I also keep a cache of hunting supplies, ammo, and several other survival items. Without trying to sound apocalyptic, getting to your BOL might just be the first phase of survival. Your BOB covers the first 72 hours, your BOL should sustain you long term until you are able to reestablish yourself back at home.

SUMMARY

Clearly, there is more to consider than just a BOV. Hurricanes, floods, tornadoes, terrorists, wildfires, plagues, and foreign invaders will show you no mercy. None of these disasters will pause while you argue about where to go or whether or not to take Freckles the Ferret with you. Survival is not about guarantees—there is always a gamble and the disaster typically has the house advantage. The only way to increase your odds of living is to plan and prepare in advance. A thorough understanding of the four facets of a Bug Out will drastically improve your chances of survival.

17 BOV RESOURCES AND AT-HOME EXERCISES

BUILDING A BUG OUT VEHICLE requires three main areas of preparation: Bug Out appropriate gear, features and accessories; information and knowledge; and hands-on practice. I have divided this chapter into a variety of BOV-related supply categories. Under each category I have listed the following three headings:

Gear Resources: Under this heading I have listed many of the Bug Out Gear items mentioned in this book along with where you can purchase them.

Further Study: Under this listing I include a variety of resources for more in-depth study of that particular category. These resources can be books, Web-sites, organizations, schools, etc.

At-Home Exercises: Practice makes perfect. It's important that you know how to use the gear and tools in your Bug Out Bag. This heading lists important At-Home Exercises to familiarize yourself and your family with key Bug Out tools and skills.

BOV SURVIVAL SUPPLIES
Bug Out Bag Resources

I highly recommend not purchasing a preassembled Bug Out Bag. Building your own personal Bug Out Bag can be a time-consuming process, but it's important. Preassembled kits are designed to make the most mar-

gins possible for the manufacturer. Often, this means including inferior (or less) gear. That isn't a reassuring formula for a kit designed to provide one with three days of survival supplies. Rather than provide retail sources for preassembled kits, I will only provide resources for further study on this topic.

Further Study

- My first book, *Build the Perfect Bug Out Bag: Your 72-Hour Disaster Survival Kit*
- willowhavenoutdoor.com: Many free articles about Bug Out Bags
- homereadyhome.com: Great Bug Out Bag for beginners blog series
- www.youtube.com: Search "bug out bag"

At-Home Exercises

- If you haven't already, start building a Bug Out Bag. Start with the six most critical categories: Shelter, Water, Fire, Food, First Aid, and Self-Defense.

BOV SHELTER
Gear Resources
Rooftop Tents

- www.arbusa.com
- www.cascadiatents.com

Shelter/Trailer Combinations

- www.campausa.com
- www.vmioffroad.com

Further Study

- None

At-Home Exercises

- Go camping with your BOV and spend at least one night in the shelter option you've chosen. Evaluate weaknesses in the plan and make changes accordingly.

BOV WATER
Gear Resources
Bulk Containers

- frontrunneroutfitters.com
- www.rotopax.com
- www.relianceproducts.com
- www.waterbrick.org

Further Study

- Emergency disinfection of drinking water: water.epa.gov/drink/emerprep/emergencydisinfection.cfm
- Water storage tips: www.ready.gov/water and www.yoursafetyplace.com/STOREFRONT/content.aspx?idcontent=56

At-Home Exercises

- Go camping with your BOV and use only the water stored in your BOV for cooking, hydration, and hygiene. Evaluate weaknesses in the plan and make changes accordingly.

BOV FIRE
Gear Resources
Ignition Devices

- www.lightmyfire.com
- www.kodiakfirestarters.com

Store-Bought Tinders

- www.zombietinder.com
- www.ultimatesurvival.com

Ready-to-Burn Store-Bought Logs

- www.duraflame.com

Further Study

- Make your own fire tinder: willowhavenoutdoor.com/general-survival/the-best-fire-starter-money-cant-buy-pet-balls-dryer-lint-fire-starter and willowhavenoutdoor.com/featured-wilderness-survival-blog-entries/how-your-underwear-and-a-pop-can-could-save-your-life

At-Home Exercises

- Go camping with your BOV and use only the ignition devices and fire tinder in your BOV to start the fire. Do not bring firewood. Use only the tools in your BOV to gather and process firewood during your campout. Make changes based on the experience.

BOV FOOD
Gear Resources
Long Term Food Options: Dehydrated and open-and-eat meals
- www.wisefoodstorage.com
- www.mountainhouse.com
- www.survivalacres.com
- www.mrestar.com
- Bulk Food Containers: www.uline.com
- Many outdoor camping retailers and websites

Cooking and Food Preparation Tools
- Many outdoor camping retailers and websites
- Metal mug/cup: www.gsioutdoors.com
- P-38 can opener: Local Army/Navy surplus stores
- Esbit stove and fuel tablets: www.campmor.com, search "esbit"
- Canister stoves: All backpacking stores and websites
- Tabletop propane stove: www.coleman.com
- Spork: www.rei.com

Further Study
- Make your own MREs: willowhavenoutdoor.com/featured-wilderness-survival-blog-entries/diy-bug-out-meals-ready-to-eat

At-Home Exercises
- Mark the expiration date of your BOV food and make that a weekend to go camping. Eat only the food packed in the BOV using only the food preparation tools in the BOV. Make changes based on the experience.

BOV FIRST AID AND HYGIENE
Gear Resources
First Aid Kits, Hygiene Products, and Tools
- Disaster medical kits: www.MedCallAssist.com and www.chinookmed.com
- Variety of Medical Kits: adventuremedicalkits.com
- GO Anywhere Toilet Kits: www.cleanwaste.com/go-anywhere-trial-pack
- Waterproof dry bags: cascadedesigns.com/sealline
- Containers: www.uline.com

Further Study
- www.redcross.org

- Disaster hygiene tips:
  emergency.cdc.gov/disasters/
  foodwater/

At-Home Exercises

- Use your BOV first aid kit to treat the next family first aid issue. Did you have everything you needed? Are there any changes that need to be made?
- While on a camping trip, do not use public restrooms or outhouses. Try using the bathroom as if in a Bug Out Scenario and those facilities aren't available. What did you learn?

BOV MAINTENANCE
Gear Resources
Tire-Related

- Spare tire mount:
  www.warriorproducts.com
- Multi-Use Jack:
  www.hi-lift.com
- Patch kits, aerosol tire inflators, and 12-volt air compressors: www.fixaflat.com

Battery Related

- Solar trickle charger:
  www.autozone.com

Key-Related

- Magnetic hide-a-key: local hardware stores

Tools and Miscellaneous

- Reactor Hard Knuckle Gloves:
  www.hatch-corp.com
- Prepackaged emergency kits:
  www.bellautomotive.com
- Fire extinguishers and mounts: h3rperformance.com
- ResQMe Seatbelt Cutting and Window Shattering Emergency Key Ring: www.resqme.com

Further Study

- Vehicle repair manuals:
  www.haynes.com

At-Home Exercises

- Know how to change a flat tire.
- Know how to change all the belts in your BOV.
- Know how to jump a dead battery.
- Know how to push start a manual shift vehicle.
- Hide an extra set of keys in a hide-a-key case on your vehicle.

BOV OFF-ROAD TRAVEL
Gear Resources

- Off-road tires:
  www.intercotire.com
- Air intake snorkel:
  www.ruggedridge.com
- Brush guards:
  www.roadarmor.com

- Four-wheel drive conversions for vans: www.quigley4x4.com
- USA Made Shovels and Wrecking Bars: bullytools.com
- Dominion Off-Road Accessory Bars: JeepSWAG.com
- GoTreads traction aid: www.gotreads.com
- Winch: www.ruggedridge.com
- The Renegade tow rope: www.bubbarope.com
- IPF 968 Series Off-Road Lights: www.arbusa.com

Further Study
- How to use a Hi-Lift Jack, an off-road winch, come-along, or pry-jack: www.hi-lift.com.

At-Home Exercises
- Get your BOV stuck. Then get it out using your off-road tools.
- Drive your BOV off-road and get a feel for what it can and cannot do. This will help to avoid unnecessary risks in a real-life scenario.

BOV COMMUNICATIONS AND NAVIGATION
Gear Resources
- Uniden HomePatrol Portable Scanner: www.uniden.com
- Shortwave radios: radioshack.com

- Emergency hand-crank radio: www.etoncorp.com
- SPOT Satellite Global Phone: www.FindMeSPOT.com/GlobalPhone
- Midland GXT Pro GMRS Radios: www.midlandusa.com
- Battery storage cases: www.inanycase.com
- Midland Base Camp 2-Way Radio: www.midlandusa.com
- Guardian Alert CB Radio: www.midlandusa.com
- Cell phone, GPS, and handheld device mounts (RAM X-Grip): www.rammount.com

Further Study
- State-level emergency alert system policies and plans: www.fcc.gov/encyclopedia/state-eas-plans-and-chairs
- Find local emergency/medical/transit frequencies at: www.radioreference.com/apps/db
- List of shortwave radio frequencies: http://support.radioshack.com/support_tutorials/communications/swave-5a.htm
- Local HAM radio repeaters/frequencies can be found at: www.artscipub.com/repeaters
- Airport HAM radio frequencies: www.airnav.com/airports

- The National Association for Amateur Radio: www.arrl.org

At-Home Exercises

- Program and use all of your communication radios and devices. Some, such as mobile HAM radio units, must be programmed in order to use. Don't wait until a disaster strikes to figure out how to use these tools.
- Communicate with (or at least listen to) outside sources using your devices.
- Develop a unique and personal FLASH code with your Bug Out Team for basic commands.

BOV DEFENSE AND SECURITY
Gear Resources

- Under-dash-mounted holster: www.texascustomholsters.com
- Shotgun/rifle under roof rack: www.bigskyracks.com
- US Survival AR-7 .22 Rifle: henryrepeating.com
- Tornado brand pepper spray and mounting hardware: www.gettornado.com
- Crovel multiuse survival and self-defense tool: gearupcenter.com
- ASP batons: asp-usa.com
- 12-gauge perimeter alarm: www.pyrocreations.com

- Waterproof Waypoint spotlight: www.streamlight.com
- Camo netting tarp: www.camonettingstore.com
- ATV and bicycle rail mount holster: www.rammount.com
- Camouflage spray-paint: www.hunterspec.com

Further Study

- Self-defense training: massadayoobgroup.com
- ASP baton training: asp-usa.com
- Regional knife defense courses: www.thepathfinderstore.com

At-Home Exercises

- Practice camouflaging your BOV. Adjust your plan and the material you use until you are satisfied with the results.

BOV STORAGE SOLUTIONS
Gear Resources

- Buckets and gamma seal lids: uline.com and nitro-pak.com
- Vittles Vault storage containers: www.gamma2.net
- Surplus military containers: Local Army/Navy surplus stores or craigslist.com
- SealLine Dry Bags: cascadedesigns.com/SealLine

- Rooftop cargo storage solutions: www.yakima.com
- LoopRope bungee cords: www.looprope.com
- STA-BIL fuel stabilizer: www.sta-bil.com

At-Home Exercises

- Do a test run. Pack your BOV at least once with everything you plan to take on a Bug Out Journey. Make changes based on what you can and cannot fit.
- Once everything is packed as you like into the BOV, pretend that the BOV has broken down. How much can you take and what do you have to leave behind? Are you okay with the results? Make changes accordingly.

BUG OUT VEHICLES RETAILERS

- EarthRoamer: www.earthroamer.com
- ICON 4x4 Trucks: icon4x4.com
- Sportsmobile: www.sportsmobile.com
- Survivor Truck: www.survivortruck.com
- UNICAT TerraCross 52: www.unicat.net

RETAILERS FOR ALTERNATIVE BOVS

- Bug Out Pack Canoe: www.oldtowncanoe.com
- Mundo Cargo Bike: www.yubabikes.com
- Argo: www.argoatv.com
- Optibike: gearupcenter.com
- GearUp ROKON: gearupcenter.com
- KLR650 Dual Purpose Motorcycle: kawasaki.com
- Nimble Cargo Scooter: nimblescooters.com
- LT Mountain Horse Snowbike: www.timbersled.com
- Ural Gear-Up: imz-ural.com

RETAILERS FOR BUG OUT TRAILERS AND CAMPERS

- Campa Cub Trailer: campausa.com
- Four-Wheel Camper: www.fourwh.com
- VMI Offroad Xtender OX Trailer: www.vmioffroad.com
- B*O*S*S* Bug Out Camper/Trailer: gearupcenter.com

RETAILERS FOR CARTS AND WAGONS

- Exodus Cart: www.exodussolutions.net
- Trans-Port-RRR Cart: www.loomansoutdoor.com
- Guide Gear Deer Cart: www.sportsmansguide.com

SUMMARY

Choosing and outfitting a BOV can be very overwhelming if you allow it. For large tasks that may feel too big to conquer, I suggest breaking them down into manageable chunks. I call this "goal-ienteering," named after the sport of orienteering. Orienteering is a sport where you use a map and compass to navigate from point to point toward a final destination. Reaching each individual point along the way makes the final destination achievable. The key to outfitting a BOV is the same way. Rather than trying to finish the entire build at once, break it down into smaller, more manageable chunks. This book is divided by chapter into those smaller manageable chunks for this very reason. While it's impossible not to skip around a little bit, try your best to focus on one chapter/survival priority at a time. I promise this will save you time and frustration in the long haul. Good luck!

INDEX